"Praying for our kids is both simpler
important than we often realize. Insi
help you understand and live out bo
everyday life. Plus, the Scripture-insp

Michelle Myers,

"Few things in life can humble you like motherhood can. And yet, how often do we try to white-knuckle our way through it all? Read this gift of a book and learn how to clasp your hands together in a new way: in prayer and praise to the One who'll carry you through."

Hannah Anderson, author of *Humble Roots: How Humility Grounds and Nourishes Your Soul*

"Prayer comes naturally to some, but not to most. And because the words don't flow, or we think we need to follow a formula, we moms end up avoiding the most essential and transforming work we do on behalf of our kids. We don't pray. But Brooke has written a wonderful book that breaks it down and makes prayer not only feel possible but irresistible."

Jeannie Cunnion, author of *Mom Set Free* and *Don't Miss Out*

"*Praying Mom* provides the exact encouragement modern moms are searching for. The inspiring prayer examples paired with Bible verse reminders make this book a nightstand-keeper."

Rachel Wojo, author and Speak Up Ministries Growth Groups director

"As one who prays daily on the Pray Every Day show, I jump up and down with joy about Brooke McGlothlin's heart for prayer. If you long for transformation, particularly in yourself, give yourself the gift of *Praying Mom*."

Mary DeMuth, author of over 40 books including, *Building the Christian Family You Never Had* and *Ordinary Mom, Extraordinary God*

"More than a book, this is a field guide—a relatable, actionable, and priceless resource for any woman with honest questions and real doubts about prayer."

Katie Westenberg, author and speaker

"Brooke McGlothlin is a trusted voice in the world of parenting. She leads with heart, wisdom, and the reminder of the foundational difference prayer makes—for us and for the kids we love."

Sissy Goff, LPC-MHSP, counselor and author of *Raising Worry-Free Girls*

"Many Christian women struggle with their prayer life but are often unsure WHY they are struggling. Brooke fleshes out these stumbling blocks with real-life examples in order to help women move forward with grace, not shame."

Erin Mohring, cofounder, Million Praying Moms

"As an *almost* empty-nest mom of five, I wish *Praying Mom* had been in my spiritual toolbox all these years. With Brooke's encouragement, not only will you draw closer to the Lord, but you'll welcome prayer as a life-giving priority on this sacred journey of motherhood."

Jen Schmidt, author of *Just Open the Door* and Balancing Beauty and Bedlam blog

"Working with Brooke and hearing her passion for praying God's Word transformed my prayer life, and it is now one of my own passions. I can't think of any better ministry than one that teaches women how to better communicate with their God."

Gina L. Smith, mentor mom/writer at Million Praying Moms

"The humility and grace that Brooke sprinkles throughout these pages will draw readers in to discover that prayer is every bit as accessible, enjoyable, and rewarding as it is essential."

Monica Swanson, author of *Boy Mom* and host of The Boy Mom podcast

"*Praying Mom* is the prayer mentor you've always wanted from a mom who absolutely lives this message on her knees."

Stacey Thacker, author of *Threadbare Prayer*

"As a mama to four young children, my heart and mind found rest reading *Praying Mom*. The biblical foundation Brooke shares is exactly what mothers need to hear."

Maggie Whitley, author and mentor at maggiewhitley.com

"Brooke McGlothlin reaches into the heart and hard of motherhood with the encouragement of a friend and the unshakable hope of Scripture."

Becky Keife, author of *No Better Mom for the Job* and *The Simple Difference*

"If you've wanted to pray more for your kids, but you struggle to know what to pray or how to pray—or if prayer is even worth it!—you will be so encouraged by reading *Praying Mom*."

Crystal Paine, *New York Times* bestselling author, podcaster, and founder of MoneySavingMom.com

PRAYING MOM

PRAYING MOM

Making Prayer the First and Best Response to Motherhood

Brooke McGlothlin

BETHANYHOUSE
a division of Baker Publishing Group
Minneapolis, Minnesota

Published by Bethany House Publishers
11400 Hampshire Avenue South
Bloomington, Minnesota 55438
www.bethanyhouse.com

Bethany House Publishers is a division of
Baker Publishing Group, Grand Rapids, Michigan

Printed in the United States of America

Library of Congress Cataloging-in-Publication Data

Names: McGlothlin, Brooke.

Title: Praying mom : making prayer the first and best response to motherhood / Brooke L. McGlothlin.

Description: Bloomington, Minneapolis : Bethany House Publishers, [2021] | Includes bibliographical references.

Identifiers: LCCN 2020058151 | ISBN 9780764238468 (trade paper) | ISBN 9780764239076 (casebound) | ISBN 9781493431663 (ebook)

Subjects: LCSH: Mothers—Religious life. | Prayer—Christianity. | Mothers—Prayers and devotions.

Classification: LCC BV4529.18 .M3725 2021 | DDC 242/.8431—dc23

LC record available at https://lccn.loc.gov/2020058151

Cover design by Brand Navigation

Author represented by MacGregor Literary Agency

21 22 23 24 25 26 27 7 6 5 4 3 2 1

To Jamie, Meg, Erin, and Angie—the Groupies

God gave us each other in a season
when I desperately needed women who would love me
even if they didn't understand me.
You have been the hands and feet of Jesus to me
and my children so many times over the years and,
more than anyone except Cory, have watched me try to
follow the Lord in becoming a praying mom.
I love each of you so much.

Contents

Foreword

I remember my first lengthy conversation with Brooke. She had asked to meet me at a Cracker Barrel to discuss homeschooling, as she was considering it and I had been doing it for a year or so. Before that day, we had exchanged hellos and small talk at church, but I didn't really know her. I don't remember all the details of that conversation, but I do remember the intensity with which she spoke. I had no doubt that this woman could do whatever God called her to do. It was the first time I witnessed her fierce love for her boys.

A few years later, I was fortunate to have Brooke and her husband join our life group. She was quiet at first, but as a fellow introvert, I didn't take it personally. When she did begin to open up, she shared with us wisdom that was beyond her years and a passion for walking with the Lord, and I soon got to know Brooke's heart. As our friendship deepened, we talked about everything and anything—the good, the bad, and even the ugly. I sought her out for advice and, even more so, I sought her for prayer.

Brooke is a mighty prayer warrior. If she says she is going to pray for you, she will. This woman doesn't just talk the talk;

she walks the walk. She prays the prayers. She believes God will answer.

I have trouble remembering what I did earlier today, but I remember much of what Brooke has shared through prayer. She pours out her heart when she prays, and it's a beautiful thing to experience. I have witnessed her praying for many things over the past decade, but perhaps her most passionate prayers concern her children. I have seen her, when at the end of her rope, turn to the Lord and simply wait. I have seen her cover her boys in prayer at times when, to be honest, I wouldn't have thought about praying for my children.

One hot summer day we were sitting at a crowded pool. It had become one of our most common places to sit and talk. Something had happened in the pool between her younger son and another boy. I listened as she talked her son through it. Then I listened to her pray for him and for the other boy. Her praying didn't surprise me in the least, but I couldn't help but notice how her little boy snuggled into her, closed his eyes, and listened. He didn't pull away so he could get back in the water, or stare off in the distance, not really listening. I have no doubt it was because that's who Brooke is: She parents with prayer.

I have had many opportunities to pray with Brooke and have her pray over me and my family. When she doesn't know what to pray, she simply gives it to God and trusts that He will do what is best. I've also watched her go through painful times of loss and struggle. Whether it was financial, relational, grief, or any other matter of the heart, I have never witnessed her waver or deal with any of it without prayer.

These days we live six hours apart, so we don't see each other very much. But thanks to technology, we talk regularly. And one thing we do most is share prayer requests.

Brooke remains one of the most amazing prayer warriors in my life. She has made it through all the hard stuff by praying her way through it. She has helped *me* through the hard stuff by praying me through it. Whatever she does and whatever happens—Brooke prays.

When Brooke first shared the concept of this book with me, I knew reading it would be like sitting down and talking with her. I knew she would go right to the heart. I knew her words would be filled with wisdom and grace. And I knew that after I read it, the way I prayed would change. This book is a gift to its readers, just like Brooke is a gift to so many people. Her words can be a vital part of your parenting journey. All you have to do is follow Brooke's lead.

Jamie Soranno
Mom and Friend

Dear Mom

In 2019, Erin Mohring and I, after years of serving only mothers of boys at The MOB Society, formed a ministry called Million Praying Moms. It was a response to the thousands of comments and emails and messages we'd received over the years that told a sad truth: Moms weren't praying. They didn't know how. Many of them didn't feel like they could, had the time, or knew where to start. These were Christian moms who believed they should be praying, but they still weren't doing it. The results were messy. The moms we talked to felt guilty about not praying. Some knew it was affecting their lives and their mothering because it indicated a lack in their relationship with and connection to God. But they felt helpless to do anything about it because they were already so overwhelmed by other parts of life.

Prayer, one of the most important parts of Christian parenting, was being overlooked, swept under the rug, or ignored completely, and the toll it took on the hearts of moms was overwhelming.

This book, and the Million Praying Moms ministry itself, is our solution for you. It was sparked by a survey we took of these same moms asking one simple question: "If you believe you should be praying, but are not, why?" We must've hit a nerve, because we received hundreds of replies, some making it clear that moms experience deep guilt and shame over this issue. So we took those answers, and with the utmost care narrowed them down to seven of the most common struggles moms face that keep them from prayer. Each of the first seven chapters in this book represents one of those challenges, and is designed to offer you biblical truth, encouragement, and hope as you learn to pray better.

Do you worry endlessly about the influence the world will have on your children but feel powerless to do anything about it? Do you struggle to answer big questions, never knowing if what you're saying is right? Do the dirty dishes, mounds of laundry, never-ending homework, and overflowing schedules make you wish you had a game plan for parenting? Something that would never fail you and never let you down?

If so, this book is for you!

Every mom I know, if she's being honest, feels the same way . . . or at least has at some point. I certainly have. When my two children were very young, the common challenges of motherhood often left me completely overwhelmed and sometimes even hopeless. It didn't take long to realize that I did not possess the skills needed to be the kind of mom I wanted to be. I'm not talking about skills like changing a diaper or getting a child to sleep through the night (although there can be a learning curve there too). I lacked the spiritual skill set to combat the lies the enemy threw at me on a regular basis.

I didn't know how to see the world through the lens of God's Word instead of through the sticky lenses of my failures. I knew letting my emotions control my response to my kids wasn't the answer, but I didn't have the tools I needed to get them in line. Running away from the chaos—something I had a habit of doing—wasn't the answer either, but I didn't know how to get the strength I needed to press in.

But there was one thing I did know.

Many years prior to becoming a mom, I chose to follow Jesus, and I believed and had settled in my mind and heart that God's Word—the Bible—was completely and absolutely true. I had decided to stake my life on it, so when the challenges of motherhood kicked my feet out from under me and left me desperate for help, I turned to the one person I knew I could count on: God. It seems simple, and it is. I just turned to the God I knew could help me. Honestly, I'm not sure why I didn't invite Him into my mess sooner.

And so I began doing the only thing I could think of—praying and begging God to do something in my home. I didn't really know how to pray that well. I had prayed throughout my life as a Christian, but mostly the "Lord, help me remember the answers to the questions on this exam," or "Lord, keep them safe," kind of prayers. Don't get me wrong, those prayers are great. Learning to pray like that, to pray at all, was a fantastic training ground for the vibrant prayer life God would develop in me years later. But those prayers weren't enough for the mothering season of my life—a season that stripped me of my pride and caused me to ask for help more often than anything else I'd ever done.

I needed something more.

So I began a practice that would change literally everything about my life—praying God's Word back to Him.

The first time I prayed Scripture I was studying Ezekiel 36:26. I can't remember why I was studying that section of Scripture, but I do remember that when I read those words, it was as if a bomb went off in my heart. I've described it in other books, but it helped me to have a biblically correct understanding of my role as a mother for the first time: God is the One who changes hearts of stone to hearts of flesh. I get to partner with Him in that process, but He's the One who makes it happen. Period.

Before I even realized what was happening, I was praying, "Lord, change their hearts of stone to hearts of flesh" on a regular basis. I wrote that verse on a sticky note and placed it outside the doors to my children's rooms so I could remember to pray it every night before bed. I even began to ask the Lord to change my heart. Even though I'd been a believer for a long time, I was realizing that there were still lots of stony places that needed His softening touch.

The next verse or passage I remember having this effect on me was Numbers 6:24–26, which says, "The LORD bless you and keep you; the LORD make his face to shine upon you and be gracious to you; the LORD lift up his countenance upon you and give you peace" (ESV). I prayed this special prayer over my boys every night before bed, and even now, as young teenagers, they still ask for the Numbers 6 prayer before they go to sleep. I have prayed this prayer over them for more than thirteen years; it's become a beautiful staple, creating a habit of prayer in our home, and I love it.

Over time, as I searched the Scriptures for more prayers to pray over my children, several noteworthy things began to happen.

Maybe the most important of those is the fact that I became more knowledgeable about the Bible itself. I grew up in church, I knew all the Bible stories from Sunday school, and I even had wonderful times with Jesus in His Word before the boys were born. But apart from a mandatory reading of the entire New Testament for a class in college, I had never really studied it in depth. Slowly, as I begged God to show me what to pray for my boys, He began to open my eyes so I could not only pray His Word but understand it for myself. I took the time to pause and reflect on things I didn't quite understand, and I became invested in trying to see things God's way. As I surrendered more and more to the truth I found there, that's exactly what happened. Instead of focusing on the chaos and craziness of my circumstances, I began to see the world around me through the lens of the Bible, allowing it, not my emotions, to interpret my life.

I know now that what I experienced was the process of sanctification. That's a big, churchy word that essentially means my life became more and more like Christ's. Not perfect. Never perfect. Just better. As I began to apply the Scriptures to everyday things, I formed a theology for life built on God's Word. My worldview became more biblical and less personal, and in the end, I looked much more like the mom I wanted to be in the beginning.

You can too.

But I know it's a struggle.

Inside this book, you'll learn more about the journey God took me on to becoming a praying mom, find heartfelt stories from moms you may already know on some level (or, if not, moms I know you will fall in love with as they share their hearts and bare their souls as it relates to their own prayer struggles), and be challenged to look at prayer a little differently than before. Each chapter begins and ends with a contribution from one of those moms, and is followed up with two important sections. The first, Pray It Forward, summarizes some prayer tips from the chapter and gives you advice for putting them into practice. Small-group leaders may want to use these bullet points as starting points for deeper discussions.

We've also included brief prayers to help you overcome the challenge covered in that chapter and enrich your overall prayer life. At Million Praying Moms, we encourage you to pray Scripture, so in keeping with that, we also highlight four or five verses that inspire heartfelt prayers. These prayers are very practical, but they're also meant to teach you how to begin praying Scripture if you've never done it before. I urge you not to ignore these prayers or think of them as "fluff." In reality, they might be the most important part of each chapter. If you're reading this book in a small-group setting, I encourage you to pray them together as you close each week.

Part 2 of the book is called Scripture-Inspired Prayers for Today's Christian Mom, and it is packed with practical prayers that cover the range of emotions and challenges moms face. It's my favorite, and I hope you love it.

I also want to point out the appendices. The first is a simple prayer God inspired me to write a few years ago that I like to pray at the start of every day. You may want to memorize it and make it your own personal wake-up prayer. The other appendix is a guide to Christian salvation. Most moms reading this book have probably already given their lives to Christ, but if you haven't and would like to know more, check it out.

I know not every mom who reads this book will have experienced each of the seven challenges I cover inside. Feel free to use *Praying Mom* as a resource for what you are currently struggling with, but I do encourage you to read each chapter. I've tried very hard to lovingly address deep spiritual and theological issues that I believe hold many women back from living the full life God intends for them even if they haven't struggled with a particular roadblock to prayer. Because you've picked up this book, I believe God has something for you inside.

I can't wait to dive in!

Brooke McGlothlin
Million Praying Moms

Part One

7 Challenges for the Praying Mom

I Don't Know If My Prayers Really Matter

Lord, Help Me Understand My Place in Your Plan

One of the hardest things about prayer is feeling like your prayers don't really matter.

I've personally gone through several seasons when I struggled to believe my prayers mattered to God, or even that they were making it beyond the ceiling of my home. Throughout harsh seasons of personal loss, miscarriage, broken relationships, and financial struggles, I have wondered if God wanted to be good to me by answering my specific prayers. But I've also experienced just enough miraculous answers to prayer—like when my friend Stacey's husband, Mike, was literally raised from the dead, or when God protected Million Praying Moms at the very last second from entering into a partnership that would have ruined us in the long run—to know that my prayers really are worth something to God. But the most important way I know my prayers matter—that they are being used by God for something important whether I can see it or not—is because

His Word tells me so. Take a few minutes to listen to my friend Sandra Peoples's story. . . .

Years ago, we were visiting my in-laws for the weekend. My husband and older son were asleep in one bedroom, and in the other room, I was crying out to God, begging for Him to answer my prayer.

All I wanted was for my younger son, James, to sleep. It was 3:00 a.m. and he was happily playing. He had slept in the car earlier that evening, and his body decided that was enough.

Why won't you just give us sleep, God? I'm not asking for anything hard. If we sleep, it isn't going to change anything for anyone else on the planet but us. And it will be a good change! I'll be a better wife, mom, and daughter-in-law tomorrow if you let me sleep now!

Because it was three in the morning and we were visiting my in-laws and life was just hard in general, I got right to the point with God: *You gave me a son with autism, and I do my best each day for him and all of us. All I ask for is sleep. If you can't even do this, what can you do?*

When I look back now, that night stands out as a turning point for me in my prayer life. I was praying prayers that God wasn't answering. He didn't bring sleep that night. He didn't lower James's anxiety when I would pray for him during a meltdown. He didn't give James the ability to speak when I wanted more than anything for him to be able to answer yes-and-no questions. Request after request went unanswered. So I stopped praying. I thought the frustration of not getting my prayers answered would be harder than not praying at all. At least then I wouldn't be disappointed.

I coasted through our days, neither praying nor praising God. James's development was slow, so each day felt just like the day before. Each year felt just like the year before. And I tried to get through it all in my own power. I was lonely because I wasn't talking to my heavenly Father, and I was exhausted because I was trying to do it all apart from Him.

Like Sandra, I've begged God for something I could only see as good and not received the answer I was looking for. When my uncle Bob was dying, I asked God to spare him. He didn't. Ten months later, when my uncle Tom was dying, I asked God to spare him. He didn't. When we were miscarrying our third child, I asked God for a miracle. I didn't get the one I wanted. I have prayed for many good things throughout the course of my life and not received the answer I hoped for. I'm pretty sure you can relate. How many of us have prayed for our spouse to come to Christ, for a child to come to church, or for a much-needed raise? These kinds of prayers are never wrong, but they are perfect examples of "good" prayers that often go unanswered, and for some of us, this can be the beginning of heart-level problems with God.

Raise your hand if it's happened to you.

Truthfully, when we're asking for something that is inherently good—like someone's salvation, healing, enough food to eat, money enough to pay bills, or, like Sandra, sleep—and we don't get it, it can make us question whether or not God *himself* is actually good. And if the devil can make us question our position as children of God, he can destroy our ability to lead others to Christ.

We pray for something that truly seems good. He doesn't give it. Doubt creeps in ("If you can't do this good thing, what *can* you do?"), and we begin to lose trust in the God who really can do anything but doesn't seem to want to. Hang with me a second, because this is super important. When we start questioning God's goodness to us, it causes a cyclical breakdown of our affection for and trust in God, and if WE don't trust Him, we can't help others trust Him. THIS is the enemy's master plan, because it prevents the spread of the gospel, and we have to guard against it at all costs. If I don't believe God is worth following, I'm sure not going to tell you to follow Him. See what I mean? Protecting ourselves from getting to this place requires that we understand it for what it actually is—a basic, heart-level error in our understanding about who God is and our place in His creation.

First, we aren't the ultimate judge of what is good, or even how the word *good* is defined. I don't like that. If I'm being honest, I like to feel I'm intelligent enough to be able to define what's good and what's not, but as it turns out, this isn't actually true (one of many things I like to believe about myself that doesn't prove true when measured against God's Word).

As humans, we can only see in part. God sees the full picture of how He is going to work all things together for good. In fact, sometimes we call things good that aren't, or that hinder what God is trying to accomplish long-term. Consider Peter in Matthew 16:21–23. In these familiar verses, Jesus is beginning to talk to His disciples about going to Jerusalem. He specifically tells them He is going to make His way to the place they think He should avoid, and that when they get there, He will suffer, be killed, and then be raised again. Peter—our stubborn, impulsive Peter—doesn't like this plan and tells Jesus he'll never let it happen. In Peter's mind, protecting Jesus is good. In his mind, keeping Jesus safe furthers the kingdom. Suffering (dying, in Peter's mind) would only hinder God's plan *as he understood it* for the Messiah. But look at Jesus' response to Peter:

> Jesus turned and told Peter, "Get behind me, Satan! You are a hindrance to me because you're not thinking about God's concerns but human concerns."
>
> Matthew 16:23

Wow. I read that passage just the other day as I was studying and praying through the book of Matthew, and I did a double take. Allow me to say it again here for the sake of emphasis: In addition to calling Peter SATAN (I mean, if that wasn't enough!), Jesus said, "You're a hindrance to me because you're not thinking about God's concerns but human concerns." Ouch. Could our beliefs about what could or should be good in our circumstances hinder the bigger plans of God? Peter truly believed that what he was standing up for, what he was praying for, what he was a part of, was good. But it wasn't God's definition of good for the Savior. In fact, keeping Jesus from going to Jerusalem and suffering would have been very, very bad . . . for all of us. In *Gospel-Centered Mom*, I described it this way:

> In every circumstance of life, we can look at what God is aiming to accomplish from two possible perspectives—either temporal or eternal. One is to seek out the immediate purpose for our current circumstances. We say to the Lord, *Why are you letting/not letting this happen? Why am I going through this? I need to see the right-now purpose for my pain/discomfort/hardships!* The second and far more important perspective is to consider the much bigger, without-end purpose of God. It involves all we can't see and a grand, overarching purpose that has existed for all time. God's full, forever-and-ever-amen purpose has

more to do with His glory than our wants and desires. . . . There's more than just now.[1]

When Sandra was begging God to let James sleep—something that truly isn't a bad thing to pray for—she was only seeing the temporal. God asks His children to keep their eyes on the eternal. I don't say this to insinuate that God doesn't care about the tender requests of mothers with their children, only that desperation makes seeing the eternal extremely difficult. Maybe part of the reason God hasn't answered Sandra's prayers for James the way she has wanted over the years was so someone reading this could be encouraged to press on. She has a story to tell of God's faithfulness that He can use to comfort others, and *that* is part of His plan for her and for James. We just don't—can't—see the end. Friends, it's called faith for a reason.

Second, if we believe God isn't being good to us by answering our "good" prayers, we're going to get cynical and stop believing God answers prayer at all. Or maybe we'll just stop believing He answers *our* prayers. That might be worse. Causing God's children to stop believing Him at His Word is the oldest trick in the book, dating back to the garden of Eden. According to pastor J. D. Greear, "Satan's go-to tactic in our lives is to break the hold the word of God has on us. So, he takes what God has declared and casts doubt on it. Satan puts question marks in your life where God has put periods."[2]

God IS good (gracious, kind, and merciful). A number of Old Testament and New Testament verses declare it to be so (Exodus 34:6–7; Exodus 33:19; 2 Chronicles 30:9; Psalm 31:19; Psalm 34:8; Psalm 84:11; Mark 10:18; Romans 2:4, to name a few). In addition to that, He declared His creation good, and He declared you (humanity) *very* good (Genesis 1). But if we have an incorrect understanding of our role in God's plan, or even that there is a bigger plan than what we can see, we'll question, and that's exactly what the enemy hopes we'll do.

That's why it's so important to understand what God's Word actually says about prayer and the part we play in it—so when those seasons come that make us question, we can quickly do what Jesus did when He was being tempted in the desert: Look at the tempter and confidently say, "It is written . . ."

The *only* way I have found to force myself to see the eternal instead of the temporal, to be able to handle it when God doesn't give me something I think is good, is to know His true character. And to do that, I have to know His true Word. In this chapter, we're going to look at two things God specifically says about prayer that should impact how we feel about it . . . even when ours don't seem to be getting answered.

God Told Us to Pray

The Lord's Prayer might be one of the most familiar prayers of all time. Straight from the mouth of Jesus and found in the gospels of Matthew and Luke, this prayer is instructional in nature. The disciples asked Jesus how to pray, and He responded by giving them this model meant to help them (and us) understand the relationship between the Creator and His created. I'm going to write it out in the King James Version. I memorized it that way when I was young and attending vacation Bible school one summer, and it just feels right coming out that way, but you can study it in any version that suits you.

> After this manner therefore pray ye: Our Father which art in heaven, Hallowed be thy name. Thy kingdom come, Thy will

> be done in earth, as it is in heaven. Give us this day our daily bread. And forgive us our debts, as we forgive our debtors. And lead us not into temptation, but deliver us from evil: For thine is the kingdom, and the power, and the glory, for ever. Amen.
>
> Matthew 6:9–13 KJV

Yes, the most basic reason to pray is because we're told to.

Actually, there's less of a directive in the Bible to pray and more an assumption that out of the overflow of thanksgiving to God, we'll be compelled to—want to—pray.

There are countless examples of prayer throughout the Old and New Testaments—prayers of thanksgiving, prayers of desperation, prayers of intercession (asking something of God on behalf of others), and prayers of adoration (telling God how amazing He is)—from Isaac, to Hannah, to David, to Solomon, to Nehemiah, to Job, to Daniel, and many more. We're told to "pray without ceasing" (1 Thessalonians 5:17 ESV), "pray and not lose heart" (Luke 18:1 ESV), "call upon [God] in the day of trouble" (Psalm 50:15 ESV), and to "pray about everything" (Philippians 4:6–7 NLT). We're given more examples than instruction for how to pray in the Old Testament. God's people modeled for us how to celebrate God's blessings, ask for God's help, stay strong in the face of temptation, and even how to understand ourselves in comparison to the God of the universe using words that offer limitless inspiration for creating, crafting, and developing our own prayers. It paints a beautiful picture of God's saints in healthy communication with Him, but it's the New Testament writings that teach us about the mechanics of prayer—why we should pray and how we should do it—and from these verses, we can only assume that God intended for His people to pray.

> "Rejoice in hope; be patient in affliction; be persistent in prayer" (Romans 12:12).
>
> "Pray at all times in the Spirit with every prayer and request, and stay alert with all perseverance and intercession for all the saints" (Ephesians 6:18).
>
> "Don't worry about anything, but in everything, through prayer and petition with thanksgiving, present your requests to God" (Philippians 4:6).
>
> "Devote yourselves to prayer; stay alert in it with thanksgiving" (Colossians 4:2).
>
> "Therefore, I want the men in every place to pray, lifting up holy hands without anger or argument" (1 Timothy 2:8).
>
> "So Peter was kept in prison, but the church was praying fervently to God for him" (Acts 12:5).
>
> "Is anyone among you suffering? He should pray. Is anyone cheerful? He should sing praises. Is anyone among you sick? He should call for the elders of the church, and they are to pray over him, anointing him with oil in the name of the Lord" (James 5:13–14).

These are just a sampling of the verses in the New Testament that seem to instruct us on some element of prayer, almost assuming that if we're Christians—followers of Christ—we're already doing it on some level. There are more, but this is enough to make the point: We're told by God to pray. More than that, we were made for prayer. Why? Because we were made for God.

Pastor and teacher Timothy Keller says, "Prayer is simply a recognition of the greatness of God. To fail to pray . . . is not to merely break some religious rule—it is a failure to treat God as God."[3] From the beginning, God walked with His creation in the garden, talking with them and communicating His heart for them. And now, even though sin kicked us out of the garden, and our relationship with God has changed, He still walks with us because He is IN us—His Holy Spirit dwelling inside the heart of the believer. God wants relationship with His children, and He's ordained prayer to be the main way it happens.

On a very simple level, the Christian life is about obedience to God—doing what He says. I know it doesn't always feel super holy to sit down and pray as a means of checking off your spiritual to-do list for that day, but it's my experience that committing to a life of prayer, and therefore a life of obedience, every single day, even on days my heart doesn't feel in it, is right. Most often, when I take a step of obedience in faith that I'm doing the right thing, my heart follows, and I find my prayers don't end up as mechanical as they started. But what about the importance of our prayers? What role do they play in God's bigger, eternal plan?

God Says Our Prayers Are Important

I think it's important to acknowledge there is a mystery that surrounds prayer that even the most advanced theologians (the opposite of me) would admit. None of us understand entirely how it works, why it works, when it works, or when it doesn't. Much holier, more theologically advanced men and women than I have admitted to feeling stumped at the mystery of prayer and how it partners with God's eternal plan to accomplish His will. But it does. Somehow, our prayers help usher in the plans of God, both now and in the end times.

Many people I know wonder why we should even bother to pray if God is sovereign and already knows what will happen to us. It's a valid question. If God is in control, why bother to ask Him to do or change anything? I think the answer to this is simpler than we want to make it, and it refers back to the section you just finished reading: because God has given our prayers the power to partner with Him in fulfilling His plans.

When I was just learning to pray, I often found myself thinking about people or situations and, despite my best efforts, was unable to get them out of my mind. It felt a little obsessive (not something I really wanted to share with other people who might think I was creepy or weird), but I did share my experience with a close friend one day, and that friend suggested something that revolutionized my prayer life . . . well, all of my life: Maybe I was thinking about these people because God wanted me to pray for them?

The whole episode reminded me of the story of young Samuel in 1 Samuel 3. Remember with me the precious story of a mom who told God she would do *anything* to conceive a child, even give him back to God to live away from her all of her life. A mom who fulfilled her promise once that child was born, giving him to the service of Eli the priest. One night, as Samuel and Eli tried to sleep, something profound happened.

> One day Eli, whose eyesight was failing, was lying in his usual place. Before the lamp of God had gone out, Samuel was lying down in the temple of the LORD, where the ark of God was located. Then the LORD called Samuel, and he

> answered, "Here I am." He ran to Eli and said, "Here I am; you called me." "I didn't call," Eli replied. "Go back and lie down." So he went and lay down. Once again the Lord called, "Samuel!" Samuel got up, went to Eli, and said, "Here I am; you called me." "I didn't call, my son," he replied. "Go back and lie down." Now Samuel did not yet know the Lord, because the word of the Lord had not yet been revealed to him. Once again, for the third time, the Lord called Samuel. He got up, went to Eli, and said, "Here I am; you called me." Then Eli understood that the Lord was calling the boy. He told Samuel, "Go and lie down. If he calls you, say, 'Speak, Lord, for your servant is listening.'"
>
> 1 Samuel 3:2–9

My friend suggested the reason I couldn't get people or events out of my mind was because God was calling me. Specifically, He was calling me to pray for those people, or the events, I couldn't stop thinking about. So I started listening, praying. They weren't always elaborate, beautiful prayers. Sometimes they were short, "Lord, please make a way," prayers. But there were also times when what I did could only be described as interceding on someone else's behalf.

I remember using one entire hourlong drive from Roanoke to Lynchburg, Virginia, to my graduate school classes for the day, to pray for dear friends who were in the middle of a divorce. I begged God to work a miracle on their behalf for an hour, and I'm relatively sure people who passed me still talk about the crazy lady they saw screaming at someone in her car who wasn't there. But God *was* there, and praying this way—paying attention to how God was speaking to me—ignited a passion in my heart for prayer that has never gone away. I still often pray myself to sleep at night by simply quieting myself and allowing God to bring someone or something to mind, and then covering them in prayer. Once one person is done, I wait for the next to pop into my mind, and cover them . . . and so on, and so on, until I fall asleep. None of those people ever asked me to pray; I just let God show me who needs prayer, and then pray.

I believe this is the practice of partnering with God to accomplish His will in the lives of these people. I don't know how it works. I don't know why it works. And I don't always know what His will is in each situation. I just know that God calls me to pray for certain people at certain times. It isn't my job to know why or how. It isn't my job to control or worry. It's just my job to pray. Somehow, God uses it.

If God already knows what will happen, and has ordained me (you?) to be a part of making it so, isn't that one of the highest honors of life? Knowing that God already has a plan, or even believing He *will* fulfill His promises, doesn't make me stop praying; it makes me pray all the more. I don't have to understand. I just have to pray. As Marshall Segal wrote,

> Prayer warriors pay close attention to the promises of God. They patiently persist in prayer by clinging to His words, as if letting go would ruin them. His promises do not become excuses to relax and pray less, but give them confidence and urgency before the throne. They know their next prayer might be the very means God has appointed to keep His promise, demonstrate His power, and display His worth. They do not draw near to God without a promise, and they refuse to stay away long *because* of what He's promised.[4]

Let's hear the rest of Sandra's story.

After so many nights of asking for sleep and not getting it, after praying for help and not getting it, I was guilty of the sin of ungodliness. When I did pray, I stuck to safe prayers that started with, "Your will . . ." "Your plan . . ." and, "Your purpose . . ." I didn't want to demand what God wasn't willing to give. I didn't want to be disappointed.

But in God's mercy and grace, He drew me back to himself. He led me to a passage that reminds me He cares about what's truly on my heart and mind:

> And they came to Jericho. And as he was leaving Jericho with his disciples and a great crowd, Bartimaeus, a blind beggar, the son of Timaeus, was sitting by the roadside. And when he heard that it was Jesus of Nazareth, he began to cry out and say, "Jesus, Son of David, have mercy on me!" And many rebuked him, telling him to be silent. But he cried out all the more, "Son of David, have mercy on me!" And Jesus stopped and said, "Call him." And they called the blind man, saying to him, "Take heart. Get up; he is calling you." And throwing off his cloak, he sprang up and came to Jesus. And Jesus said to him, "What do you want me to do for you?" And the blind man said to him, "Rabbi, let me recover my sight." And Jesus said to him, "Go your way; your faith has made you well." And immediately he recovered his sight and followed him on the way.
>
> Mark 10:46–52 ESV

Did you notice Bartimaeus's safe prayers? "Have mercy on me!" he cried out twice. Like my safe prayers, Bartimaeus was asking for something he could already have: God's mercy. If he didn't ask for what he really wanted, then he wouldn't be disappointed if Jesus didn't deliver. But Jesus called him closer and asked, "What do you want me to do for you?" This is what I felt Jesus asking me as well. What is it that you really want?

I don't want to stop praying just because my requests aren't answered in the time and way I want them to be. I don't want to stop asking for things only God can do. I don't want to play it safe every time I talk to my heavenly Father. The Jesus who asked Bartimaeus to come closer, the Jesus who asked him what he really wanted, is the Jesus who now sits at the right hand of God interceding on my behalf.

In Bartimaeus's life, it was his blindness that kept him from following Jesus. So Jesus made a way, as we see in verse 52: "And immediately he recovered his sight and followed him on the way." I don't want my disappointment in unanswered prayers to keep me from following Jesus, to keep me from having a relationship with Him that grows stronger each day. Jesus will do for me what He did for Bartimaeus—He will make a way.

It starts with this passage in Mark, with the Holy Spirit guiding me here to stop and praise God for the specific love He has for me. And it will continue each day as I pray for mercy, for grace, and for His will, but also specifically for money to cover James's therapy costs, for opportunities to serve and encourage more special-needs families this year, for sleep, and for help.

How is your prayer life, friend? Have you grown safe (or distant, or quiet, or angry)? Follow Bartimaeus's example with me. Move closer to Jesus and tell Him what you truly want. Be restored in your relationship with Him.

Pray It Forward

» Remind yourself that feelings aren't facts. We don't like feeling that God isn't answering our prayers, but in truth He is, in His ways and in His timing.

- » Admit your struggle and ask others to pray for you and over you. Borrow from their faith when yours is weak.
- » Work on your belief that God is only good if He gives you what you want. That is a prosperity-gospel distortion of the truth, not the actual truth.

Prayers

Verse: "I am the vine; you are the branches. The one who remains in me and I in him produces much fruit, because you can do nothing without me" (John 15:5).

Prayer: Father, I am forever connected to you, even when I don't feel like my prayers matter. Help me to remember this truth even when I can't feel it, and to bear much fruit for your kingdom as I join you in accomplishing your plans through my prayers. Make me more sensitive to your calling. In Jesus' name.

Verse: "And not only that, but we also boast in our afflictions, because we know that affliction produces endurance, endurance produces proven character, and proven character produces hope. This hope will not disappoint us, because God's love has been poured out in our hearts through the Holy Spirit who was given to us" (Romans 5:3–5).

Prayer: Father, it's hard to ask you to help me rejoice when things go wrong. But I believe there's a purpose in all you allow. Prove to me that hope doesn't disappoint. Pour out your love in my heart today and every day as I seek to follow you.

Verse: "And my God will supply all your needs according to his riches in glory in Christ Jesus" (Philippians 4:19).

Prayer: Father, I can't always see your provision with my own eyes. Help me to believe that the way you choose to answer my prayers is what's good and best for your eternal plan.

Verse: "They came to Jericho. And as he was leaving Jericho with his disciples and a large crowd, Bartimaeus (the son of Timaeus), a blind beggar, was sitting by the road. When he heard that it was Jesus of Nazareth, he began to cry out, 'Jesus, Son of David, have mercy on me!' Many warned him to keep quiet, but he was crying out all the more, 'Have mercy on me, Son of David!' Jesus stopped and said, 'Call him.' So they called the blind man and said to him, 'Have courage! Get up; he's calling for you.' He threw off his coat, jumped up, and came to Jesus. Then Jesus answered him, 'What do you want me to do for you?' '*Rabboni*,' the blind man said to him, 'I want to see.' Jesus said to him, 'Go, your faith has saved you.' Immediately he could see and began to follow Jesus on the road" (Mark 10:46–52).

Prayer: Father, I want to see. I want to believe that you are the God who makes the blind see, the lame walk, and the dead rise to life. I want to be a part of your amazing, eternal work here on earth. Jesus, Son of David, have mercy on me and make me see!

I Don't Know What to Pray

Lord, Teach Me to Pray Your Word

In the introduction of this book, I shared the story of how I became a praying mom, so I won't repeat it. But you should know that I'm assuming some things about *you*. First, that you believe in God, or you believe that there's someone bigger and stronger than you who can be prayed to when you need help. I don't expect that only Christians will read this book, but I hope your heart will be a little bit more open to Jesus after you're done. If you need help knowing what that means, please see appendix 2, or reach out to me or the ministry of Million Praying Moms and we'll help you know what to do.

I'm also assuming you know you can't do this life thing without some help . . . at least not do it well. Hopefully you've realized that you don't have to have it all together, don't have to be enough, and aren't strong enough to manage all the things the world would call you to do. If so, even though it might feel like the very worst place to be, I promise, you're right where you belong.

Finally, I'm assuming you want to pray, or believe on some level you should be praying more than you are, but just don't know how, or what, or when. In this chapter, I'd like to teach you about my very favorite way to pray, and why I believe it's the best way to pray. But first, let's hear from my dear friend Teri Lynne Underwood as she shares her prayer story.

I've felt like a prayer failure.

I know—that sounds crazy for someone to say in a book about being a praying mom, especially someone who has written not one but two books about prayer. But it's the truth. Prayer has never come easily to me. I'm a do-er kind of girl, more comfortable with a checklist than with contemplation, and prayer always felt so, well, boring. For more years than I'd care to admit, my prayer life was mostly about making a list of people and situations and asking God to be over all of it. Which isn't wrong, but somehow it felt like it wasn't really what prayer was meant to be.

As if being a prayer failure isn't enough, you should know that I'm also a fourth-generation pastor's wife and a Bible teacher. People assumed I was a prayer guru and often even asked me how to pray. I'd mumble through answers I'd read in books, hoping they'd never figure out I wasn't actually confident in this area.

Once I got pregnant, something shifted, and I was desperate to know not only HOW to pray but WHAT to pray. The weight of motherhood moved me to my knees, but I still wasn't sure what it looked like to pray with purpose and power.

I did what former college debaters do and researched prayer. I read books and wrote down quotes. I printed prayer guides and studied prayer methods. I set up prayer journals and organized prayer cards.

I did everything I could think of except actually pray.

Even with all the resources at my disposal, I just didn't feel very sure about what I was doing. And more than anything, I didn't want to pray the wrong way or for the wrong things.

My desire to pray was strong, but my desire to be the right kind of pray-er was stronger, and it paralyzed me. My quiet time continued to consist of 98 percent of my time in the Word and 2 percent of my time making a prayer list.

As I was studying my Bible one morning, I read this verse: "Let my cry reach you, LORD; give me understanding according to your word" (Psalm 119:169). A switch flipped, and I realized I had everything I needed to know about what and how to pray right in front of me in Scripture.

Two truths, in particular, led me (Brooke) to praying Scripture as my main vehicle of conversation with God.

The first is from Hebrews 4:12, which says the Word of God is "living and effective and sharper than any double-edged sword, penetrating as far as the separation of soul and spirit, joints and marrow. It is able to judge the thoughts and intentions of the heart." The second is from Isaiah 55:11: "So my word that comes from my mouth will not return to me empty, but it will accomplish what I please and will prosper in what I send it to do." If those two verses were true, and I believed they were, then it seemed to me that there could be no better thing to pray than God's Word itself!

There is an intimate link between God's Word and prayer. We need both in order to be adequately prepared to face the world.

A famous quote by the nineteenth-century preacher George Müller says, "Only a life of prayer and meditation [on God's Word] will render a vessel ready for the Master's use." So often we see prayer and spending time studying the Bible spoken of at the same time, maybe even interchangeably, and that's because they are both valuable—or better, invaluable—spiritual disciplines that work together beautifully. When Teri Lynne had her "aha" moment inside of Psalm 119:169, it was because her eyes were opened to the beauty of praying God's Word back to Him.

Most often, when we're praying for something, it's because we have a lack in some area of our lives. A situation exists that we can't explain, can't fix, or don't have the answers for. But God's Word IS the answer. To everything, all the time, and in every way. I know that seems presumptuous. You might be thinking, "I'm pretty sure the cure for cancer (or fill in the blank with another issue that isn't specifically mentioned) isn't in the Bible," and you'd be right. There are lots of things we deal with today that aren't mentioned verbatim in God's Word. As I write this, the world is in the middle of a pandemic, and, as far as I know, there is no written prescription for a cure in the Bible. But you know what is in the Bible? How to handle the challenges of seriously stressful life events, the promise of God's provision, and the correct worldview for enduring in the midst of chaos. It also tells us how we should treat other people, take care of the sick, and put others' needs in front of our own. It's all there, and suddenly, as God opened her eyes at just the right time, Teri Lynne knew that the best way to pray was just to pray God's Word, letting it teach her the right way to think and interpret the world around her.

Any time we don't know what to pray, how to pray, or when to pray, we can simply go to God's Word. The promise we have from God is that His Word is alive. It isn't like other books out there, even this one. The Message version of Hebrews 4:12 says it like this: "God means what he says. What he says goes. His powerful Word is sharp as a surgeon's scalpel, cutting through everything, whether doubt or defense, laying us open to listen and obey." I find that this paraphrase really helps the meaning of Hebrews 4:12 hit home for me.

God's Word will teach you everything you need to know about whatever you're praying for. Also, according to Isaiah 55:11, His Word does exactly what He wants it to, because it's living and active, and it is constantly at work in us, or can be if we spend time studying it. If God says, "I want my Word to do (fill in the blank) in (insert a name)'s heart on this day and year," you can bet it will. Because God's Word is always true and always right, it will never fail when He plans to use it. These are the two main reasons I choose to allow God's Word to shape and direct my prayers on a regular basis, but there are more. Let's look deeply at six reasons God's Word should be our gold standard for prayer.

1. It's what we're taught to do in Scripture.

Or maybe it's better to say that it's one way we see God's people praying in Scripture. Jesus taught us a lot about the heart of prayer in Matthew 6:9–13, commonly called the Lord's Prayer. I mentioned earlier that I memorized this as a child, and it still brings me comfort. It teaches me to think about my posture before God (God is God in heaven; I'm not); reminds me that God's will is what I should be praying for (not my own); gives me the tools to ask for what I need each day (and not get ahead of myself); helps me remember to ask God for forgiveness as well as offer forgiveness to others; and keeps me on my knees in surrender, knowing that I desperately need God to help me stand in the face of temptation, because my strength alone is not enough. These are the underlying principles we all need to keep in mind any time we're praying to our Father in heaven, but it's not the only way we can pray.

We see examples of God's people praying Scripture in the Old Testament, but I'd like to focus for a minute on a couple important, distinct examples from the New. In Acts 4, after Peter and John had been arrested for preaching the gospel, were found innocent of any and all crimes, were warned to quit preaching about Jesus and told the religious leaders they wouldn't, and were returned to their own people, they felt inspired to praise God and worship Him through prayer.

> "Master, you are the one who made the heaven, the earth, and the sea, and everything in them. You said through the Holy Spirit, by the mouth of our father David your servant: **Why do the Gentiles rage and the peoples plot futile things? The kings of the earth take their stand and the rulers assemble together against the Lord and against his Messiah.** For, in fact, in this city both Herod and Pontius Pilot, with the Gentiles and the people of Israel, assembled together against your holy servant Jesus, whom you anointed, to do whatever your hand and your will had predestined to take place. And now, Lord, consider their threats, and grant that your servants may speak your word with all boldness."
>
> Acts 4:24–29, emphasis mine

Notice the words in bold? Those represent most of verse 25 and all of verse 26, but they are also a direct quote from Psalm 2:1–2. What we see Peter, John, and the other people present at this prayer meeting doing is allowing their prayers to God to be directed by, or inspired by, a truth they know from God's Word. In this case, they're remembering the truth of Psalm 2:1–2, which asks the question, Why do people even try to rage and plot against the Lord? It's futile, because what He purposes will stand! This truth inspires them to pray the same thing for themselves in a situation where they are feeling raged and plotted against. They're asking the Lord to make this truth true in their current circumstances, effectively saying, "Lord, be true to your Word." And that, my friends, is something God always does. He is always true to His Word.

Maybe even more notable than Peter and John, Jesus himself prays Scripture while hanging on the cross. Matthew 27:46 and Mark 15:34 both record Jesus speaking to His Father in the words of David in Psalm 22:1 (ESV): "My God, my God, why have you forsaken me?" According to Matthew Henry's commentary on this verse of the Psalms, these words of lament "may be applied to David [the writer of the Psalm], or any other child of God in the want of the tokens of his favor, pressed with the burden of his displeasure, roaring under it, as one overwhelmed with grief and terror, crying earnestly for relief."[1] Jesus was using the words of David, written centuries before He walked on the earth, to convey the depth of His pain and suffering back to God. And we can too.

2. Scripture tells us to hide God's Word in our hearts so we might not sin against him.

This instruction is from Psalm 119:11. The CSB version of the Bible, which I'm really growing to love, uses the phrase "I have treasured" instead of "hidden." To treasure something means to treat it with awe, reverence, and a sense of great importance. I've often wondered, if our house were ever on fire, what treasures would I choose to grab in the mere seconds I would have to react? My children, of course. Our animals, if there was time. My grandmother's Bible, if possible. And that's pretty much it. But really, the only priority I would have would be to get my family safely out. Even family heirlooms, like my other grandmother's engagement ring, pale in comparison to the people I love most.

I think that's the way we're supposed to feel about the Bible, and the more I'm in it—studying, praying, seeking to understand and apply—the more I know I need it. This makes sense in light of John 15:4–5:

> Remain in me, and I in you. Just as a branch is unable to produce fruit by itself unless it remains on the vine, neither can you unless you remain in me. I am the vine; you are the branches. The one who remains in me and I in him produces much fruit, because you can do nothing without me.

Scripture is clear that Christians can't survive this world without staying tied to the Father, and the way we do that is through studying His Word, treasuring it, hiding it in our hearts, memorizing it, and learning how to apply it to our lives. Ironically, when life gets hard, the first thing I tend to do is pull away from reading the Bible. I wish that wasn't my true confession, but it is. During the 2020 worldwide quarantine, as well as all the other world events that took place at the same time, I found it terribly difficult to concentrate on anything at all, much less get any meat out of God's Word. I tried, but it often felt like my mind was somewhere else. Slowly, as I spent less time reflecting on the truths of the Bible, anxiety, and even some moments of panic, crept in. Every new month felt like a sucker punch just waiting to happen. Everyone experienced heightened states of anxiety and helplessness, but the people who stayed in God's Word had an unchanging, unmovable rock to stand on. Thankfully, I've been standing on that rock now for many years. I'm not advocating for leaving God's Word for any length of time. I'm not in any way saying it's okay to let distraction, well, distract us from hiding God's Word in our hearts. But I am saying that when the storms come (and they will), those who have built their homes on the Rock will not be destroyed (Matthew 7:24–27).

I once saw a documentary about a Chinese Christian who was arrested for preaching the gospel. He was brutally tortured for his faith; he endured many things you and I can only imagine (or maybe *can't* imagine) simply because he dared to tell others about Jesus in a country radically closed to Christianity. But as he told the story of his captivity, he kept coming back to the one piece of hope he clung to: Even in the darkness of solitary confinement, he was able to recite memorized passages of Scripture. Not always out loud (most of the time not out loud), but while in pain, while suffering the unimaginable, he spoke the truth of God's Word to his own heart over and over again. Nothing his captors did could take that away from him.

After many years he was released, and despite never once having a physical copy of the Bible at his disposal, his faith remained intact and allowed him to treat his captors with dignity when they showed him none.

The title of the documentary escapes me, but when I think about this man's story, two emotions hit me: 1) I'm *ashamed* at how few verses I have memorized, and 2) I'm *grateful* for the years God has allowed me to study His Word. If we're allowing it to bake and live inside of us, we will have it when we need it most. And as it does its work in us, opening our eyes so we can see things God's way more clearly, we'll become more like Christ. Not only that, but a natural outcome of praying God's

Word back to Him is that we'll begin to understand the Bible better, and that can only be good.

3. God's Word is intimately connected to His very nature.

Can I get even deeper for just a few minutes? I promise if you keep reading, you'll see this praying-Scripture thing in a totally new light.

John 1:1 says, "In the beginning was the Word, and the Word was with God, and *the Word was God*" (emphasis mine). When I'm trying to understand Scripture, I often go back to simple math. The straightforwardness of math—how there's usually only one right answer—appeals to me and helps me keep things simple. What I'm about to propose to you is anything but simple to understand, so I'm hoping that breaking it down into mathematics will help you catch the powerful imagery of the idea that the Word = Jesus = God.

The word *was* is the past-tense conjugation of the verb *to be*. Of course, the present conjugation is the word *is*, and in math word problems, *is* translates to *equals*. No difference. Of the same measure. Identical. Same thing. So in a very real way, when John tells us that the Word was God, he's saying Jesus *is* God. But he's also telling us that the Word is Jesus. Let me explain. . . .

Later, in verse 14 of John chapter 1, we read, "The Word became flesh and dwelt among us. We observed his glory, the glory as the one and only Son from the Father, full of grace and truth." There's no other way to read these verses than to see them as a declaration saying the Word of God is Jesus. I don't think it's too much of a stretch to say that you could hold out your Bible—if indeed you believe it's the inspired, 100-percent-true Word of God—and say to a friend, "Here's Jesus." Pastor and author John Piper says it this way:

> John calls Jesus *the Word* because he had come to see the words of Jesus as the truth of God and the person of Jesus as the truth of God in such a unified way that Jesus himself—in his coming, and working, and teaching, and dying and rising—*was the final and decisive message of God.*[2]

Other verses throughout the New Testament refer to Jesus as "the Word," or link following Him to the Word, but what I want us to consider is the idea that there is something very powerful about praying God's Word. We're not just praying words when we pray Scripture; we're actually praying Jesus. Notice I didn't say we were praying *to* Jesus. In a sense, we are. But what I said is that we are *praying* Jesus. And if we want to take our mathematical equation even one step further, I believe it would be correct to say Word = Jesus = God = Truth. When you're praying Scripture, you're powerfully praying God's truth back to Him in the form of His Son—the Son whose mission is your salvation and redemption, taking what's broken and making it beautiful, healing, and restoring. Jesus, "the Son he loves" (Colossians 1:13); Jesus, God's "Beloved One" (Ephesians 1:6); Jesus, the third part of the Holy Trinity, one with the Father (John 10:30). What better thing could there possibly be to pray?

4. Praying God's Word back to Him is a form of worship.

I grew up singing hymns. "Amazing Grace," "Have Thine Own Way, Lord," "I Surrender All," and "The Old Rugged Cross" were the songs of my childhood in church. When I started walking closely with the Lord in my mid-twenties, I left hymns behind and fell in love with praise and worship music. Point of Grace, Crystal Lewis, Michael W. Smith (I'm dating myself, I know), and other groups like them led me in worship most days into my late thirties, and for a season I didn't want to listen to hymns at all, mainly because I had experienced one too many services where the words to those songs—glorious and true though they are—only reached my lips and never touched my heart. Now, in my forties, there's nothing that blesses me like true worship from the heart through hymns. (I still love modern worship music too!) But there's never been one day, one minute of one day, when I didn't need to be reminded of God's truth in some way, and music is a powerful medium for helping us remember and feel deeply the truths of Scripture.

Too many churches argue over the music sung on Sunday mornings, but in my opinion, if studying God's Word is the most important thing we can do, worship is a close second. David danced before the Lord (2 Samuel 6:14), Paul and Silas sang and worshiped God while in chains (Acts 16:25), and as we studied earlier, Peter and John and their people raised their voices together in unison to worship after they were released from prison (Acts 4:24–29). But worship is more than just singing the right songs.

Worship is an attitude of the heart, a posture that recognizes Jesus as Lord. Singing is certainly a form of worship, and the Bible instructs us to do it, but worship can also be a single act of obedience, a simple day devoted to the Lord, or even an ongoing effort to think about things that are true, honorable, just, pure, lovely, commendable, excellent, or praiseworthy (Philippians 4:8). Worship is anything we do or say that acknowledges Jesus as Lord of our life, and praying God's Word back to Him is like saying, "I trust you, Lord. I believe what you say. I believe you'll keep your promises. I believe you're good. Your Word is the standard by which all other things are measured in my life. I worship you for giving me your Word." Not that God needs reminding about His promises, but that our hearts need it every day.

5. Praying God's Word is like telling your emotions to get back in line.

I find myself coming back to King David so often as I try to understand God and the world around me. He was a man who loved God and followed hard after Him, but he was also a man who royally messed up time and time again. In the Psalms, we're given a highly valuable peek into his conversations with God—good, bad, and ugly. David questioned God, praised God, fussed at God, and openly adored God all throughout this book of the Bible, sometimes all in one chapter! The psalms of David are truly a gift from God to us! Reading his prayers has taught me more about my own prayers than anything else I can think of, including how to be honest with my Creator about how I'm feeling.

Let's look at Psalm 6—one big, long, emotional prayer from David to God, often referred to as a lament, or something to pray in a time of great distress or trouble. Many of David's prayers of lament share the same format. They start with an honest reflection of what he's currently feeling and experiencing—maybe even complaining about them—then move to applying God's truth to those experiences and feelings, and end with worship because his cares have been cast upon the Lord (Psalm 55:22). He is no longer carrying his own burden, so his relief causes him to praise God. It's a beautiful example of how David was always real with God. Look at the language he uses throughout. Phrases like, "I am weak," or, "my bones are shaking," or even, "my whole being is shaken with terror." David describes his feelings and emotions using words like *weary*, *groaning*, and *eyes that are swollen from constant crying*.

In my book *How to Control Your Emotions So They Don't Control You*, I describe how David's laments often display a format for controlling our emotions. I call this "Feel, Know, Do."

> **Feel:** What we see with our eyes (our experiences and circumstances) affects our emotions and causes us to feel a certain way. Our feelings may be right or they may be wrong, but either way, as believers we're called to submit them to the authority of the Word of God.
> **Know:** Our minds remember what we know to be true (i.e., the truth of God's Word, who we are in Christ, all that's available to us because we belong to Him, God's many promises, etc.) when we invite God into our circumstances with an open heart.
> **Do:** We act on truth, not on what we can see or what we feel. What we do is affected by what we know. As David remembered the joy of his salvation, his heart turned from feelings of despair at what he could see happening in his life to feelings of hope and joy at what he knew God could do, and he acted based on *this* knowledge, not what his emotions told him was true.[3]

I can't tell you how many times this has been true for me in my own walk with God. When I come to Him honestly, raw emotions and all, and take the time to reflect on how His truth applies to my situation or who I am in Him, my emotions get back in line. As you speak or write the truths found in God's Word, it WILL transform the way you think about the world around you. It will inform how you understand your circumstances, how you treat others, and how you make decisions. And praying God's Word helps you pray absolute truth. If there's one thing I know, it's that my emotions often lie to me. They let me know something is wrong, but they also tend to tell me it's much worse than it really is. I constantly need to pause to get my emotions in check before responding to difficult—or even everyday—circumstances, and it's much harder to be swayed by our emotions if what we're praying to correct them is the truth of God's Word.

6. You'll never run out of things to pray.

Several months ago, I ran into an old friend. For about thirty minutes, we took the time to catch up and learn about what God was doing in each other's family and life. I used to see her a couple times a year, but my family recently moved back to our hometown, and our paths don't cross the way they used to. She shared about all the things going on in her life, and I shared about how The MOB Society—the ministry I co-founded with Erin Mohring years ago—had morphed into what is now Million Praying Moms. I told her our mission was to help moms make prayer their first and best response to the challenges of parenting. What she said in response to this opened my eyes and deepened my passion for prayer. She said, "Brooke, I'm so glad you're doing this. Moms need it. I need it. I have to confess that while I want to pray, and know I should be praying, I always get stuck because I don't know how, and I don't know what. Really, I just don't know where to start."

This conversation with my friend was profound for me in a couple different ways. First, it confirmed that the ministry of Million Praying Moms is needed. I still believe that prayer is the most important—but most overlooked—part of Christian parenting today, and my heart and passion is to do something about it. Second, it made me realize that struggling with prayer goes across Christian maturity levels. I had expected most of the people we served at MPM to be young Christians, but my conversation with my friend that day opened my eyes to the fact that mature Christians who have been walking with the Lord for many years struggle too.

My answer to women (and men, for that matter) across age groups, socioeconomic levels, and even Bible knowledge is very simple: Pray God's Word. You'll never run out of things to pray for, and what you pray for will almost always be right.

John Piper says, "I've said to people, 'You can pray all day if you pray the Bible.' Some people wonder how you can pray longer than five minutes, because they would lose things to pray for. But I say that if you open the Bible, start reading it, and pause at every verse and turn it into a prayer, then you can pray all day that way."[4]

Hopefully by now you can see why I've fallen in love with praying God's Word, and why it's my heart's passion to help other women learn to do the same. There is literally nothing, no other spiritual discipline, that has grown my relationship with Jesus like praying Scripture. It's a cycle of growth that starts with a mom in need who is willing to search God's Word for verses that speak to her situation, and begin to pray them in the spirit of asking God for His will to be done in her life and in that of her family. From there, it moves into an increased hunger for understanding, and the beginning of the ability to apply the truths she's finding in the Bible to her own life, changing her very way of thinking about the world around her so that she begins to look more and more like Christ. My pastor, Mike Mitchener, says, "Prayer is the number one way you develop your relationship with God."[5] This is my story. My prayer is that it will also be yours.

If the idea of praying Scripture is new to you, I've written a resource you can download for free with the code *prayingmom*; it's located inside of the Christian Mom Shop and is entitled "How to Pray God's Word." Just visit www.christianmomshop.com to get your free resource, and start praying in this powerful, profound way today. Now, let's hear the rest of Teri Lynne's story.

Praying Scripture isn't some mystical experience. Instead, I discovered it was a way for me to take all the truths and lessons I'd learned through years of study and pour my heart out to the Lord. Psalm 119 guided me to pray for deeper understanding of Scripture. From there, I spent time in Philippians, where I prayed for humility and a mind focused on Christ. I prayed for my child's identity to be rooted in who God says she is. I prayed for my church to be vibrant like the churches in Acts. I prayed for my husband to be a leader like Nehemiah.

I learned what it was to lament as I prayed through Lamentations, and prayed for my words and actions to bring honor to the Lord as I prayed verses from Proverbs.

Every day I still wrote down my list of people and situations needing prayer, but I discovered how to apply what I'd read in the Bible to those needs. I realized my prayers were, more often than not, mostly Scripture.

Over the past twenty-plus years, I've prayed through countless passages, verses, and even whole books of the Bible. I've discovered that praying this way not only enables me to pray with boldness and confidence, but also leads me to pray in areas I otherwise would have neglected.

Learning to pray has been a journey for me. I definitely don't feel like an expert, but I do have more purpose and confidence. Praying God's Word back to Him has been a game-changer for me. And as I've shared my story with others, many of them have found boldness and assurance in their own Scripture-based prayers as well.

Pray It Forward

» Highlight verses or passages you can pray for yourself and others. I use my yellow highlighter for this. For example, I have highlighted John 15:8 in my Bible as a reminder to pray that I will bear much fruit for God's glory.

» Look for prayers within Scripture that you can pray. The Psalms are full of this type of writing, but don't forget to look in other places as well. The prayers we find in the Word can help guide us to growth in our own prayer lives.

» As you record your prayer requests, make it a practice to attach verses to them. If you are praying for someone's salvation, you could use Romans 10:9 as a reminder to pray that others will believe and confess Christ.

» Make praise and adoration a key part of your prayer life. Use verses that speak of God's character as a foundation for these prayers. The Bible is replete with descriptions of who God is and what He does.

Prayers

Verse: "For the word of God is living and effective and sharper than any double-edged sword, penetrating as far as the separation of soul and spirit, joints and marrow. It is able to judge the thoughts and intentions of the heart" (Hebrews 4:12).

Prayer: Father, help me to believe that your Word is true, and make it come alive for me in a personal way. Use it to show me what I need to know, and change my opinions where they need to be conformed to your will.

Verse: "Rejoice always, pray constantly, give thanks in everything; for this is God's will for you in Christ Jesus" (1 Thessalonians 5:16–18).

Prayer: Lord, help me to see all of the many gifts you've given for which I should give thanks. Even when the hard things come, help me to thank you for walking with me through them.

Verse: "You will call to me and come and pray to me, and I will listen to you" (Jeremiah 29:12).

Prayer: Lord, help me know and believe that you hear me when I call. Use the Holy Spirit, who lives in me, to remind me to pray in all things, throughout every day.

Verse: "I call on you, God, because you will answer me; listen closely to me; hear what I say" (Psalm 17:6).

Prayer: Father, let my heart be encouraged in the knowledge that you listen. You aren't surprised by what's happening in my life, or in my children's lives. Hear my prayers and answer me according to your best plan.

Verse: "Devote yourselves to prayer; stay alert in it with thanksgiving" (Colossians 4:2).

Prayer: Father, I confess that I don't always know what it means to devote myself to prayer. More than that, I can't see how I have time. But I want to know and experience the fullness of being your child. I want to be a part of ushering in your kingdom. Give me a fresh desire to be devoted to communicating with you. Make me alert to the times I need to pray.

3

I'm Exhausted from Trying to Trust God

Lord, I Believe. Help My Unbelief.

Nestled in three of the four gospels—Matthew, Mark, and Luke—is the story of a woman who fought one single physical issue for over twelve years. And not just any issue, but one that isolated her from every good part of her community and faith experience, one that made her unclean to all her friends and family. We call her the woman with the issue of blood, and her story starts out like this:

> A woman suffering from bleeding for twelve years had endured much under many doctors. She had spent everything she had and was not helped at all. On the contrary, she became worse.
>
> Mark 5:25–26

Twelve years. Every dime gone, wasted on treatments that were humiliating and pointless. Only getting worse and worse as time went by. I can't imagine her pain. With each new doctor's visit, hope loomed. Maybe *this* would be the time, the person, the treatment that could make her pain and humiliation go away! And then, time after time, the crushing news that failure and disappointment would once again rule her life. I wonder if there was a point during those twelve years when she thought to herself, *Enough! I just can't do this anymore. I can't keep fighting this fight only to be knocked down over and over.*

I know something of that pain. Not in the same way, of course, but I've been through an incredibly trying season of life, about seven years long, where it seemed like heartache after heartache kept me from getting sure footing. During that season, we lost both of my uncles, my aunt, two grandparents, a friend in the Virginia Tech shootings, and at the end of it all, a baby to miscarriage. Seven people in seven years. I look back now and think I just might've walked through those years in a bit of a haze. Had it not been for God's Word and my amazing rock of a husband, I'm not sure how I would've turned out.

How do we keep praying, keep trusting God, when we're exhausted from trying for so long? Allow me to introduce you to my dear friend Stacey Thacker, whose prayer story will help give you the strength you need to keep going.

I made my way to the only room where I knew I could find refuge in the middle of the chaos all around me. Shutting the bathroom door and turning the lock into place, I leaned against the wall and slid down to the floor, my emotions matching my position.

Low.

Rock-bottom.

Desperate.

This small room, a prayer closet for me lately, had become my battlefield. The war going on inside my heart, which I doubt anyone suspected, was (is, truthfully) real and threatening. A few tears escaped my eyes before I wiped them away and went even lower.

Facedown on the bathroom floor is just about as low as you can go.

What brought me here and rocked my belief wasn't just one hard thing. It was walking through one hard thing but having another one show up right on its heels. The first one knocked me for a loop because it meant saying good-bye to my dad. He passed away rather suddenly after a long battle with cancer. It took a year or so of heavy grieving, but after a while, I was able to get back up, take God's Word as my banner, and keep going.

The second hard thing came about a year later and was even more devastating. Honestly, I didn't think that was possible, but it was, because this time it involved the health of one of my girls. I remember sitting in the hospital after a long night with her in the ER, wrestling hard with God and thinking, *Really? This is just too much. I can't do this right now.* Still, having learned a few things that first hard time, I reached for the Word and found my footing. It took a little longer this time.

But the third thing? And the fourth thing? Once again, I found myself facing the unknown, this time involving my husband. One night, during a business dinner, he had a sudden cardiac arrest that turned every aspect of our lives upside down. What I mean by that is my husband died for a few minutes. Medical personnel were able to resuscitate him, but we had no idea what damage had been done while no oxygen was being pumped to his brain.

Each of these events took place within a three-year period.

If I'm being totally honest, I'm not made of the right kind of stuff to be able to handle that much hard in that short amount of time. Even though I know where to go for hope and help—I've done it so often before—I'm exhausted from trying to trust God and wondering what it is finally going to take to empty me of *me* so He can quit allowing hard things in my life. So here I am. Facedown on the bathroom floor, clinging to the same hope I always have, and questioning whether I'll be able to leave the bathroom floor anytime soon. I kind of doubt it.

I had the privilege, and I use the word *privilege* with great care, of watching Stacey walk through this threadbare season of her life. In fact, when her father passed away suddenly, and later, when her husband, Mike, literally died and was brought back to life, I was one of the first people she reached out to. Stacey and I have the kind of relationship where she knows if she needs prayer, I'm going to pray for her. And pray I did.

As Mike was fighting for his life, before we even knew if he would make it, God led me to create a prayer group for the Thackers on Voxer, a walkie-talkie-like app we often use to communicate with friends in business and ministry. Stacey has been a faithful friend and cheerleader to so many women who give of themselves to help spread the gospel to other women and children, and I knew they would want to be praying for her. So I reached out to everyone who knew Stacey within our ministry circle and asked them to join the prayer group. We ended up with over thirty women, and I knew God would use our prayers to provide for the Thackers somehow. What I wasn't prepared for was how God would use that group in such a powerful way that I think it might forever rank up there as one of the most profound seasons of prayer I've ever experienced.

My kids had just started full-time in school, and we were at the beginning of our move back to our hometown, so this mom, who had spent all of her mothering years homeschooling up to that point, found herself with time. Most of it I spent working, but when Mike was in the hospital, I was able to devote myself to prayer and fasting for them in a new way. I can't tell you how many mornings during the two to three weeks we actively prayed for the Thacker family that I found myself walking around my house, interceding in worship on their behalf. Our group of mighty prayer-warrior women would share songs with each other, and then we would worship together in our own homes using those songs, some of us spread apart by a distance of thousands of miles. The words to those songs were, to us, our way of battling for the Thacker family in prayer. The words became our anthem, our battle cry. It might seem odd to think of a work-at-home mom walking around her house in her slippers after dropping the kids off at school, waving her hands in the air and singing prayers to God at the top of her lungs, but if you can picture it, that's pretty much what I looked like. (And we had no curtains on our windows in the kitchen! I really don't know what the neighbors think of me. . . .)

If the concept of singing a prayer is new to you, think about the Doxology sung in many Christian churches.

> Praise God, from whom all blessings flow
> Praise Him, all creatures here below
> Praise Him above, ye heavenly host
> Praise Father, Son, and Holy Ghost.
> Amen.

The word *doxology* simply means a study of praise, or a way for the people of God to collectively offer praise to God by speaking or singing truth back to Him. Doxologies were prominent in Old Testament times, and Jesus would've heard them chanted or sung as a part of normal, everyday Jewish worship. There are, of course, many more doxologies traditional to the Christian faith, some of them quoting Scripture word-for-word, and most of them end with *Amen* or *Amen and amen*. Why? Because we're offering them as a prayer to God. We're saying, in effect, "Lord, please let this be." If you think about it this way, singing prayers doesn't seem so weird after all . . . even if you're doing it in your pajamas.

This group of prayer warriors the Lord gathered together read Scripture to each other, prayed that Scripture together, sang to each other on that crazy Voxer app, taught each other what God was showing us in the Scriptures on behalf of the Thackers, and challenged each other to go deeper in prayer, all because we loved our friend dearly and wanted God to do a miracle on her behalf. And He did.

I want to stress that we didn't know exactly what the miracle would look like. Our persistent prayer was that God would breathe full life back into Mike Thacker. We wanted him to live. We begged God to heal him so that Stacey could have her husband, and their four girls could have their father. God chose to answer that specific prayer, but I would still be testifying about the powerful God we serve who used the prayers of His daughters to usher in a miracle even if that miracle ended in Mike being taken home to be with Him.

Healing comes in more ways than life here on earth. Mike's ultimate healing, and ours, will come on the other side of heaven, and we have to keep that knowledge at the forefront of our minds as we ask God for what we want. It wasn't wrong for us to ask God for healing *here*, but it would've been shortsighted of us to think it might not have been God's plan to offer ultimate healing *there*. As much as we wanted God to keep

Mike here, we realized that "we are members of a family, and it's not just [the Thackers] God is engineering for. We are part of a flock, and [God] has the entire flock in mind."[1] We must guard against thinking that just because God doesn't answer our prayers immediately, or the way we want Him to, He doesn't care. It's just that He cares about everything, all of His flock. His promise to do what is best for us is tied inextricably to what is best for the ushering in of His kingdom. More on that later.

One Saturday evening, when things looked most grim for Mike, Stacey Voxed me individually and said the doctors had done an MRI and found little to no brain activity for Mike. She was devastated and asked me to keep praying. I prayed all night long. Into the wee hours of the morning, God woke me from sleep to keep praying. The next morning, I got up to go to church with my family. I shared what was going on with our Sunday school class, who prayed for God to heal Mike and provide for Stacey, and then went on with the rest of class and the worship service. After church that day, we decided to stay for a potluck, and when I got to the basement of the church, I realized I had a new message from Stacey. I stepped outside to listen as quickly as possible and was blown away as she told me that the doctors had done another MRI that morning and Mike had brain activity! After that point, things began to turn around rapidly for Mike, and today, he is a walking, talking, breathing example of a miracle of God. He went from death to life, and I believe God used the desperate prayers of about thirty women to usher in the beginning steps of his healing.

That whole story, at least my side of it, sounds amazing, right? It kind of makes you want to jump up and down and yell, "YAY, GOD!" and yell we did. Mike truly is a miracle, and I truly do feel like God used our prayers as a part of His plan to do it. My story sounds great, but Stacey's experience of this story was dramatically different. Even though her community surrounded her, and even though God answered our prayers for Mike to be healed and live, she's still the one who had to live it out, and she continues to live it out in a way I never will. In her book *Threadbare Prayer*, she tells the story of even more hard things that happened in the middle of this very, very hard thing:

> On this particular day, I was torn in two. I needed to be with [my husband], but also at a different hospital in town with our 10-year-old daughter. She had a treatment scheduled that day. Her illness had reared its ugly head in the days before her daddy landed in his own hospital bed. We could not postpone and I needed to be the one to take her. And so, I stretched thin and took her.[2]

The business of doing life can be exhausting, and there's more to the story that we won't tell here. Even the post-miracle healing process can require everything we have.

Let's go back to our woman with the issue of blood. The rest of her story, beginning in verse 27, goes like this:

> Having heard about Jesus, she came behind him in the crowd and touched his clothing. For she said, "If I just touch his clothes, I'll be made well." Instantly her flow of blood ceased, and she sensed in her body that she was healed of her affliction. Immediately Jesus realized that power had gone out from him. He turned around in the crowd and said, "Who touched my clothes?" His disciples said to him, "You see the crowd pressing against you, and yet you say, 'Who touched me?'" But he was looking around to see who had done this. The woman, with fear and trembling, knowing what had

> happened to her, came and fell down before him, and told him the whole truth. "Daughter," he said to her, "your faith has saved you. Go in peace and be healed from your affliction."
>
> Mark 5:27–34

I honestly don't know why God made this poor woman wait twelve years to get her healing. I don't know exactly why God allowed my family to go through so much loss, and I can't explain with much authority why God allowed Stacey's family to suffer the way they have. I know some families, some people, who don't get the healing they've prayed for until they're completely healed in heaven. But I do know this: God wants us to keep praying and trusting Him through our hard times, even when we have to ask Him for help to do it. If you asked Stacey, I'm sure she would tell you there were plenty of times of doubt, times when uncertainty crept in and she lost faith, especially when she thought she had given all she had and God asked for more. We all lose faith sometimes, even if it's short-lived, but the ones who will keep believing, keep praying, keep pressing forward, and keep asking God to help them when they can't do life alone are the ones who leave the biggest impact on this world for Christ.

When our lives get hard—when it feels like we can't possibly keep trusting God even for one more minute because we are totally and completely worn-out from the exhaustion of it—we can ask God to give us what we need to do it again. When our strength runs out, and even before, His strength is made perfect (2 Corinthians 12:9).

As Christians, we are tasked with comforting others with the comfort we've been given (2 Corinthians 1:4), and friends, the world is watching to see if we'll share. I tell my boys all the time that their friends are watching them to see if the God they say they serve is worth serving, especially in the hard things. I remind myself of this often when I'm around my own non-believing friends. When life is difficult, the world expects us to walk away, give up on the God we say is big enough to handle it all, but this is the time when we must not walk away. Instead, we can choose to sit down and wait for God to show up for us. He will, because it's HIS name at stake in our lives, not our own.

My friend Gina Smith (whom you'll hear from later in this book) messaged me the other day and said, "I was reading Psalm 23 yesterday, and something stood out to me that I don't think I've ever seen before. When I read verse 3, 'He refreshes and restores my life; He leads me in the paths of righteousness for His name's sake,' the words that stood out were, 'for His name's sake.' I realized that I want to be refreshed and restored and led because I am tired! I am weary. I want to know what to do next. I want Him to do it for *my sake*. This reminded me that He does refresh and restore and lead, but it is for *His name's sake*, not for my comfort. Yes, it does benefit me. I do get refreshed! But it is ultimately so I can continue being used for His purposes and His glory!"

This is the best kind of hope we could possibly wish for! There is nothing God is more dedicated to than glorifying His own name! We can bet our lives on the fact that God will do whatever it takes to make His name known, and in the process, we get to benefit. He comforts us, refreshes us, and restores us so that we can be used again *by* Him to lead others *to* Him. God won't leave us without relief because He needs us to be restored in order to use us to further His kingdom. What good news!

In Mark 9, we see the story of a father bringing his young son to Jesus. The disciples couldn't heal him from the spirit that made him have seizures and foam at the mouth, so he asked Jesus if He could do anything. Jesus replied, "'"If [I] can"? Everything is possible for the one who believes.' Immediately the father of the boy cried out, 'I do believe; help my unbelief!'" (Mark 9:23–24).

I do believe. Help my unbelief.

That's the prayer of a hurting Christian. The one who is holding on by a thread, who dares to look up one more time in faith and believe that God is working, even in the hard things. The world is watching us, friends. Lord, help our unbelief so that the world will be drawn to you!

Now, let's hear the rest of Stacey's story.

One piece of truth has given me hope throughout every hard trial and kept me tethered to God when I was too exhausted to keep going:

Jesus is praying for me.

I'm sure His prayers are a good deal better than my coming up with any words that make sense from the bathroom floor. The ache as I reached for Him in those dark days was deeper and wider than I ever would have imagined it could be back when that first hard thing hit my heart. Still, I know there is power in declaring truth over my weary heart, even when I feel I can't. So I vocalized my belief and affirmed to my own heart that God is good, that He is near, and that He has plans for me. I also recognized that all these hard things are making me like His Son. God is chipping away at the pieces of my life that don't belong.

I've been reminded recently that God often asks us to trust Him in the midst of our impossible places because He can—ask us and be trusted, that is. In 1 Kings 17:7–16, there is a story of a widow who was down to her last bit of meal and oil. She is collecting sticks to make one last loaf of bread for her son, as any mother would do, and believes this will be their last supper.

God sends Elijah the prophet to her in that very moment, and he asks her for a drink of water and a bit of bread.

"I don't have any bread. I'm starving," she responds.

Elijah says, "Bring me your last loaf. Have faith. You will not run out in this impossible place."

In the middle of her fledgling faith, God asks for even more.

What kind of God asks a widow for her last bit of bread?

The One who rains down bread from heaven.

The One who is the Bread of Life.

The One who is able keep a jar of flour from ever reaching empty.

> So she proceeded to do according to the word of Elijah. Then the woman, Elijah, and her household ate for many days. The flour jar did not become empty, and the oil jug did not run dry, according to the word of the LORD he had spoken through Elijah.
>
> 1 Kings 17:15–16

Still sitting on my bathroom floor, I find the cure for my unbelief in the One who finds us in our hard and impossible places, gathers us up, prays for us, asks us to trust one more time, and is able to sustain us without bread if need be. I remember that every time I have met Him here, in this lowest place, He has never failed to answer my cry for help.

My threadbare prayer as I get back up, wash my hands, and open the door is, "*Lord, I believe. Help my unbelief.*"

And He does.

Pray It Forward

» Know the Word. Interviewed for the book *Hope for the Weary Mom*, Tracey Lane, a mom who lost her only son in the Virginia Tech shootings, said the one thing that made the most difference in her ability to handle that horrible loss and heal from it, was that she had spent so many years leading up to it building her life on the firm truth of God's Word. Know the Word.

» Declare truth over your heart. It isn't enough just to know the truth of God's Word. When you're going through something hard, you have to ruthlessly apply it. This means you might have to choose to believe God's truth over what you can see, hear, taste, or touch over and over again until you believe it.

» Remember God's faithfulness. I suggest making a list of all the ways God has provided for you and keeping it in your Bible, so that when hard things come—and they will—you can pull it out and use it to help fuel your belief in His ability to do it again.

Prayers

Verse: "In the same way the Spirit also helps us in our weakness, because we do not know what to pray for as we should, but the Spirit himself intercedes for us with inexpressible groanings. And he who searches our hearts knows the mind of the Spirit, because he intercedes for the saints according to the will of God" (Romans 8:26–27).

Prayer: Jesus, I'm too tired to pray, and I wouldn't know what words to pray if I could. With all the belief I can muster, I'm choosing to have faith that you are praying for me right now.

You know what I need. Search me and make a way for me to take the next step. In Jesus' name.

Verse: "Immediately the father of the boy cried out, 'I do believe; help my unbelief!'" (Mark 9:24).

Prayer: Father, I believe. I can't ever go back to not believing in you, not knowing that you are my Savior, the One who holds me together. But I'm struggling to believe right now, so please help me in my unbelief to trust you in even this.

Verse: "Now faith is the reality of what is hoped for, the proof of what is not seen" (Hebrews 11:1).

Prayer: Father, please don't let my hope in you be put to shame. I can't see how you'll provide, but I'm choosing to believe you will. In Jesus' name.

4

I Don't Believe God Hears My Prayers

Lord, Help Me Learn to Trust You When I Can't See

In September of 2011, my husband and I lost our third baby to miscarriage.

It was an early pregnancy loss, I was only about six or seven weeks along when it happened, but it was a significant loss nonetheless. In the days after the miscarriage, I chose very carefully whom I would speak to about it. I have never felt so closed off to those around me. The topic seemed like sacred ground, and talking about it with just anyone cheapened it somehow in my heart and mind, at least for a time. Mainly, I just shared my innermost thoughts and feelings with my husband. I stepped back from writing, speaking, and, really, everything for a season. But as with all kinds of grief, the world went on, and so I had to, too.

I'm sure on the outside I looked okay, but the truth is that I wasn't. The miscarriage loss came on the tail end of several other significant losses in our life, and I truly think it was the last straw. It was also what God used to bring me to the end of a long battle against myself. To make matters harder, three of my dearest friends were all pregnant at the same time. Even today, when those three little boys are running around playing together, I see a hole where mine should have been. It really felt, for a short time, as if God wanted to be good to everyone around me, except me.

I had a lot to learn.

My friend Gina Smith, who is one of the wisest women I know, is going to tell us her story of loss, and how she felt God had abandoned her prayers in one season of her life.

• • ✻ • •

Over the past few years, my husband and I have faced some circumstances that have left us very weary. After we worked and ministered on a college/seminary campus for over twenty-five years—the place where we had lived and raised our children; where we had lived life with and cared for literally hundreds of college students and young couples; where I had gone to college and Brian had gone to seminary; where we met, dated, and married; this place that held so many memories and history; where so many relationships had been nurtured; and where every single one of our God-given gifts had been used . . . the place that we thought we would be serving for the rest of our lives—the college came to a point where it could no longer sustain itself financially, and it was forced to close.

There had been signs that things were not going well financially. We prayed for a miracle, fully expecting God to do something extraordinary, but for reasons we may never know, the miracle never came. When the day approached for the doors to permanently close, we sat in my husband's office, numb and in disbelief. "It's over," I sobbed. "I can't believe that it's really over!"

In the months to follow, we weren't sure how to pray. Those around us had no idea how deeply this was affecting us. "Brian can just find another job!" they would say, but they didn't understand that our life on that campus was much more than a job to us. It had been our life's ministry. Very few were able to understand our suffering. We felt disoriented. Not knowing how to pray, I would sit on my couch and just whisper His name, "Jesus . . ."

We were left living on a quiet, empty campus that was once filled with life and purpose. Brian was hired by the new owners, so we were not forced to leave the home we'd lived in for so many years, but we decided to continue working on that campus until God provided another job—and we hoped that provision would happen sooner rather than later. We tried to remain faithful with each day that we had been given, but the underlying feelings of grief and loss of purpose were a constant force trying to pull us down into unbelief, and they were attempting to weaken our faith in God.

Soon after all of this took place, we faced the death of our biggest support system and cheerleaders when both of my husband's parents passed away within two years of each other. My in-laws had been the most consistent people in our lives. No matter what happened in our lives or in theirs, they were there. They were patient with us when we got married and were learning to function as a young couple, and again after we had children and were learning to be parents, and they were never offended if we made a choice they didn't understand. They simply and generously did everything they could to support and love us. They loved our children and did all they could to attend piano recitals, soccer games, volleyball matches, graduations, and birthdays. They supported us and encouraged us in any way they possibly could. Their deaths left a gaping hole in our lives that can never be filled.

Two years later, both of our children were married a year apart. The loss of ministry, the loss of our precious parents, and then our children getting married left us feeling that almost everything that had given us purpose had suddenly disappeared. We felt as though we had been stripped of all we were confident in, and it felt as if God were no longer listening to the cries of our hearts. I have compared this time in our lives to a computer that crashes—it loses all of its data and has to be rebuilt. We felt as though we had crashed, and we began to ask God to rebuild and show us what He wanted for our future.

I wish I could be sitting down in front of you over coffee (or your favorite hot beverage) while we have this talk, because I think it might hurt a little in the end, and I've found that hot beverages make hard conversations easier.

Years ago, I trained volunteers in the basics of counseling so that they could serve women in unplanned pregnancy, a job that was very important to me. One of the things we really emphasized with these lay counselors was that you have to earn the right to confront someone. This is true in the counseling room, and it's true in life. It's much easier to challenge someone's views about themselves, their decisions, beliefs, and even actions when you have some kind of relationship with them. If you don't, you might get more than you bargained for (believe me, I know this personally). You and I don't know each other, so I'm banking on the hope that you've heard my heart throughout the chapters preceding this one, and that by now you feel comfortable with me and believe I really do care about you. I pray I've earned your trust, and therefore have earned the right to talk about some hard things about us as women in this chapter. If not, I apologize for not having more time to build our relationship, but I won't apologize for all I'm about to say, because it's the truth. Hang with me for a while? I think we'll come full circle and that you'll probably still like me when we're done. I'll start by asking this question:

What is it we're really communicating when we say, "I don't believe God hears my prayers"?

To answer that question, I'd like to take a look at several of my favorite authors who have written about or spoken on the topic of prayer—both men and women. Some of the people we'll sit down with in this chapter are alive today while others have been gone on to heaven for many years, but they all have something in common: They're passionate about prayer and passionate about God. That, in my opinion, makes them worth listening to. Together, we'll allow them to bring us to a place where we can answer the question above.

Prayer Is a Reordering of Loves

In his book simply titled *Prayer: Experiencing Awe and Intimacy with God*, pastor and teacher Timothy Keller tells the story of how he became a man of prayer. Having taught the Word of God for many years, and prayed for many things throughout his lifetime, he and his wife came to a season they knew they wouldn't survive without going deeper in prayer. Sickness, combined with devastating world events that impacted them personally, forced Tim and his wife to study prayer for themselves so they could have a deeper understanding of what it is and how it works. I always find the best work on a topic is written by someone who has lived through it.

Most problems with prayer start with love. Or, more specifically, our inability as sinful humans to love God more than we love ourselves. As Tim and his wife dove into the subject of prayer in God's Word and volumes written by learned biblical scholars, they found they knew very little of the fullness of what can be ours as believers because of prayer. It starts with how much—or how little—we love God.

Several years ago, I got to hear Beth Moore speak at Liberty University. In her inspiring, challenging talk to future leaders in the church and for God's kingdom, she asked this question, which I paraphrase:

"Do you love God? I'm not asking you if you love to worship God. I'm not asking you if you love to study God's Word. I'm not even asking if you love God's Word or love to teach God's Word. I'm asking you if you love *God*. Are you so grateful for the way He saved you, changed you, and has blessed your life with His presence that you are forever in love with Him for the sake of Him? Because if you're not, this Christian life will tear you apart. You'll question Him, be confused by Him, even hurt by Him as the years of your ministry go by. If you don't love Him, you'll walk away, but if you do, you'll be able to withstand whatever storms may come."

According to Tim Keller (and I believe Beth Moore would agree), "Living well [depends] on the reordering of our loves."[1] Notice Tim doesn't say the reordering of our *lives*. The reordering of our lives will happen naturally and beautifully as we reorder our *loves*.

So I'll ask these questions: *Do you love God? What do you love more than God?* Can I answer from my own heart? As I look at my life, it becomes clear that I often love financial security more than God. I always struggle to trust God in this area of our lives, wishing my husband and I had more in the bank to cover us if and when a crisis comes. When we're low on funds, I'm afraid. When we're well into the black, I feel safe. More than once—actually, more than one hundred times throughout my adult life—I've had to remind myself that God himself is our personal banker, and that He will provide all we need. Throughout my adult years, God has proven himself faithful, but it's a lesson I always seem to have to learn the hard way.

Sometimes I love being liked more than I love God. My husband and I have made many decisions for our family over the past fifteen years that look different from the decisions of those around us. We've been questioned for choosing to homeschool our children through grade school. I was actually told I was going to ruin our children by homeschooling them! We've been isolated, ignored, and generally looked at like we each have two heads for trying to make our Christian faith the biggest part of our family's life. I have been accused of having vain motives for writing and told that I try too hard to understand how God wants us to raise our boys. The challenges and misunderstandings we've endured just for trying to follow God's leading for *our* family have been difficult, and caused me to get sidelined many times by having to heal from my broken heart over not being liked. I'm just that person who feels it deeply when people don't like me.

But one of my biggest struggles is loving my kids more than I love God—and I bet most of us can say that, if we're honest. When I first started praying seriously for my boys, especially when I started praying God's Word for them, I believed God would change them instantaneously. Why I believed that remains a mystery. There's certainly no evidence that God is bound to do what we ask right when we ask it in the Bible. In fact, more often God asks us to be vigilant and persistent in prayer, choosing to use the bigger picture to accomplish His exact plan instead of ours.

In the early days of becoming a praying mom, I dealt with a persistent frustration with God for not doing what I told Him to do, when I told Him to do it, especially because I knew He could. In fact, I think that's one of the hardest things about trying to believe God is always good. We know He can snap His fingers and fix our mess, big or small, but He doesn't often choose to do it that way. Instead, He chooses to get in the mess with us and teach us how to walk with Him through it. As a mom and as a self-professed control freak, I don't like that. I want Him to do what I think is best for my children right now. I can look back on my own life and clearly see that the hard things I went through shaped me and made me more open to my need for a Savior, but I don't want my boys to have to go through that. No loving mother does. What I want is for God to make them have the devotion of fully grown men when they're teenagers, but life just doesn't work that way, does it? At least not very often.

It may have taken me several years to see my own heart's weaknesses this way, but they certainly aren't news to God. I like how Tim Keller put it: "God is the only person from whom you can hide nothing. Before him you will unavoidably come to see yourself in a new, unique light. Prayer, therefore, leads to a self-knowledge that is impossible to achieve any other way."[2]

Ephesians 1:18–19 says:

> I pray that the eyes of your heart may be enlightened so that you may know what is the hope of his calling, what is the wealth of his glorious inheritance in the saints, and what is the immeasurable greatness of his power toward us who believe, according to the mighty working of his strength.

Keller explains, "To have 'the eyes of the heart enlightened' with a particular truth means to have it penetrate and grip us so deeply that it changes the whole person. . . . Nothing but prayer will ever reveal you to yourself, because only before God can you see and know your true self."[3] I don't know that I would ever have known these things about myself—*really* known them enough to ask God to change them so I could see things His way—if I hadn't become a praying mom who learned to pray the Scriptures.

Prayer Is a Lifeline to Hope

Corrie ten Boom was a Dutch Christian who was arrested for hiding Jews in her home to help them escape the Holocaust during the Second World War. Corrie, her father, and her sister Betsie were all arrested. She and Betsie were sent to Ravensbruck, the concentration camp where they were both subjected to unspeakable cruelty, and where Betsie died of starvation. In *The Hiding Place*, Corrie tells their story of God's faithfulness, how they learned forgiveness, and how those horrific circumstances taught them to pray. Of Betsie's experience in the camp, Corrie says, "More and more the distinction between prayer and the rest of life seemed to be vanishing for Betsie."[4]

What in the world does that mean?

Only that the more intense Betsie's experience, and the more difficult her circumstances, and the more challenging they were to her faith, the more she prayed.

I'm an introvert, and relationships can be hard for me. At the most, I have only three or four close friends at a time. I've always envied people who have a large support group, but that just hasn't been my experience, or really, when it comes down to it, my preference. I much prefer a small group of close friends, and I'm much better one-on-one than I am in a group. As I mentioned before, I sometimes love the idea of being liked more than I love God, and often struggle with feeling like people probably don't like me, even before I've given them a chance to try! Silly, I know, but the real me.

Several years ago, when I attended a conference, this habit of mine came to a head. It was a leap of faith to go in the first place, because I didn't know that many people. I really like having someone to hang out with when I'm at retreats or conferences, but I found myself without one for this conference. I walked down the hallway to an after-dinner session where I knew I had no one to sit with, and the fear of being alone, or, more accurately, *looking* alone when everyone else seemed to be in their group of people, overwhelmed me. All I could think to do was pray, so that's what I did. Right there, in the hotel hallway, to myself, I began to pray, *I am loved by the King. I am valued by the King. The King gives me His worth. I'm a daughter of the King. Lord, help me remember I'm not alone because you're always with me.* I said those things over and over again until I could *feel* that they were true. And that's the key. What's happening around us will make us *feel* like God isn't good or doesn't want to be good to us, but the truth is that He always, always is.

Of course, my circumstances—having the privilege of attending a conference where I learned how to use my gifts to help others grow in Christ—were absolutely nothing like what Corrie and Betsie ten Boom endured, but the principle is the same. Betsie learned to pray and tell herself the truth even while everything around her told her there was no hope, so the line between the time Betsie spent in prayer and the time she spent doing everything else blurred. Betsie had learned the secret to praying without ceasing (1 Thessalonians 5:17), the secret to praying to get more of God himself, not just to get what we want.

Prayer Is Submission to God's Plan

Ruth Graham wanted to be a missionary. Her parents were medical missionaries to China, and seeing devastation, disease, and dysfunction during her childhood years convinced her all the more that people needed Jesus. Her dream was to be a single missionary to Tibet, but that all changed when she met and married a good-looking boy from North Carolina named Billy. Billy's calling was to be an evangelist, sharing the gospel with millions, and after much prayer, Ruth decided her calling was to serve Billy.

Can you imagine a woman today making that sacrifice? In essence, Ruth laid down her dream—what she thought was right for her life—and picked up God's dreams—what He had purposed for Ruth Bell Graham throughout all of eternity. On prayer, she said, "Men of God whose prayers are recorded for us in the Bible never read a book on prayer, never went to a seminar on prayer, never heard a sermon on prayer. They just prayed."[5] And that's what Ruth did too. When faced with a fork in the road of her life's mission, she chose to pray and ask God what she should do. She chose the path He had for her instead of the one she had always wanted, and God used her in behind-the-scenes ways to impact millions of lives for the gospel.

If you had asked me what I wanted to do with my life when I was in college, or even grad school, being a work-at-home mom juggling motherhood with writing and running a small ministry would not have been on my radar. Much more likely you would've heard me say I wanted to have my own counseling practice, a PhD, and a career teaching at the university level. You guys, if you could see how far my life is from that original dream, you'd just snort. I promise, you'd laugh so hard, you'd snort. My vision of my forties was high heels, briefcases, and lectures. My reality is comfy Toms, jeans, and online meetings where you're bound to hear loud kids and barking dogs. I do still wear fancy earrings. And I actually started my PhD before we had kids. But I got two classes in before we got pregnant with our first son, and I was so sick with him in the first trimester that I never went back, dropping one dream for another . . . or at least putting it on hold.

I was able to share that story with that son in a recent conversation and help him see how following God doesn't always look like we think it's going to. We had been talking a lot about surrendering to God's plan for his life, and he was concerned that being a Christian automatically meant God was going to deny him the things *he* wants to do, but I was able to help him see that God uses our dreams, and any progress we make on them as we follow Him, as a part of the bigger plan. I wanted to help people, so I thought I had to be a counselor. I wanted to teach people, so I thought I had to be a professor. I might not technically be a counselor with my own practice, but I use my education with every book and article I write. I might not technically be a professor, but every time I type something and hit *publish*, I'm given the opportunity to teach others what Jesus has taught me. It's not that God didn't allow me to follow my own dreams. He just had different plans for how they would play out. I shudder to think what I would've missed if I had insisted on my own way.

Prayer Is about Faith

You might be wondering, four chapters in to this book, why I haven't given you clear, step-by-step action points on how you can create a discipline of prayer when you don't already have one. I will. I'll share some of the practical steps I have implemented in my own home and heart over the years and throughout the various seasons of my children's lives. I'm also hoping that the verses and prayers at the end of each chapter, and the Scripture-inspired prayers in part 2, will help jump-start your prayers. But there's a specific reason I haven't given you a list of things to do yet, or hands-on ways to kick-start your prayer life. Get ready, though, because we're starting to move into that hard conversation I told you about at the beginning of the chapter. Ready? Let this quote from pastor Jon Bloom set in: "Prayerlessness is not fundamentally a discipline problem. At root it's a faith problem."[6]

If we can't pray, won't pray, don't have time to pray, or don't believe God hears our prayers, the problem is one of faith. And as with all problems of faith, the issue lies in our hearts. Somewhere there is a breach or break in our relationship with God, our understanding of His truth, or our pursuit of a biblically accurate purpose for our lives.

I don't think it's too much of a stretch to say that if you're not praying, you're missing out on the maturity God wants to give you as a believer. Please understand, I'm not saying people are not believers if they don't pray. Jesus equals salvation, and Jesus alone, but my heart hurts for what people are missing, the freedom and healing they aren't getting, the joy they aren't experiencing because they're not praying.

A few years ago, someone close to us passed away suddenly and tragically, throwing our family into grief, disbelief, and shock. I felt almost desperate to somehow ease the pain our loved ones were suffering, but there wasn't really anything I could say or do to make it better.

The Monday after the funeral, I woke up early while my boys were still asleep, but I felt like I couldn't even get out of bed, like there was an invisible weight pulling me down and telling me to stay under the covers. I fought the weight out of bed, to the bathroom, to the kitchen where I got a cup of coffee, and then as I sat down at my kitchen table to stare at my Bible. I knew—because I've spent years getting to know God—that the answers to my physical and emotional heaviness were inside. Hope was in there. I actually heard a voice in my head say, "What you need is in that book," but my hands felt too heavy to reach for it. I'm not sure how long I sat there and stared at the navy-blue leather cover, listening to that voice tell me to reach out and open it, but after some time had passed, I finally opened my Bible to Psalm 40 and uttered this simple prayer: "Jesus, would you come?"

> I waited patiently for the Lord,
> and he turned to me and heard my cry for help.
> He brought me up from a desolate pit,
> out of the muddy clay,
> and set my feet on a rock,
> making my steps secure.
> He put a new song in my mouth,
> a hymn of praise to our God.

Many will see and fear,
and they will trust in the LORD.

Psalm 40:1–3

These brilliant words from David aren't meant to be a platitude, or an empty promise. I think they're a method for overcoming . . . a method for experiencing God in every single place, every season, every circumstance. Sometimes we just need to ask Jesus to come, and then sit and wait for Him. Literally sit and wait while He sorts out what is weighing us down. He will, you know. . . .

If we're crying, He will turn and hear.

If we're in the pit, He will bring us up.

If we feel unstable, He will give us a sure foundation.

If we've lost our joy, He will give us a new song, and it will be one of praise to Him.

So I waited patiently for the Lord. I approached God's Word with heaviness, hurt, and overwhelming loss, but praise God I left His Word that day with joy. I felt the heaviness lift as God's Word was living and active in me (Hebrews 4:12). This is what God's Word, combined with a simple prayer, can and *will* do if we choose to go to it. But if we choose not to, well, obviously it won't.

So I'm being a truth-teller, and praying it comes across in love. If you find yourself in a time of prayerlessness, ask yourself where the breakdown is. Go after it. Get right about it. Fix it. Ask Jesus to come.

Prayer Is about God's Kingdom, Not Ours

Elisabeth Elliot was a missionary, author, teacher, and mother and the wife of missionary and Christian martyr Jim Elliot.

Jim, four other men, and their wives and families answered God's call to take the gospel to the Auca Indians of Ecuador in the 1950s. As you may know, all five of the men—Jim Elliot, Ed McCully, Roger Youderian, Pete Fleming, and Nate Saint—died at the hands of the Auca, speared to death as they tried to make face-to-face contact with them. Later, Elisabeth returned to the Auca, actually living with them along with their daughter, Valerie, in an effort to continue the work she and Jim had felt called to. I've read that Elisabeth never sought the spotlight, but because of her experience and faith, God certainly brought it to her. Elisabeth died in 2015, and in her eighty-eight years on this earth, she authored over twenty books and spoke numerous times to women, leading them in a closer, more active faith in God. If God gives me enough time, I will make my way through her entire library before I get to heaven myself.

As it related to the death of her husband, Jim, and the other men killed that day, Elisabeth shared that all five wives prayed without ceasing leading up to the day they died, and begged God for mercy that very day until they knew their prayers had been answered. You might read that and question the use of the words "until their prayers had been answered," because after all, didn't God say no to their prayers? Hadn't they asked—begged—God to bring their husbands safely home from that trip into the jungle? One could say God didn't answer their prayers, or that He somehow didn't *hear* their prayers, but He did. As relayed by Elisabeth, the missionary Amy Carmichael once said, "Isn't 'no' an answer?"[7] We just don't like to be told no.

On the topic of the Lord's Prayer, Elisabeth taught,

> Prayer forces me to lay all of my life before God and say, "God, here I am. All of me. For your kingdom [not mine].

Do anything you want to do with me and through me, at any cost."[8]

And isn't that exactly where our trouble lies? The answer to the question we posed at the beginning of the chapter—*What is it we're really communicating when we say, "I don't believe God hears my prayers?"*—is that we are upset with God for not answering them the way we think is best. When Elisabeth asked God why He didn't care enough about her to prevent her husband's death, she heard the Lord say, *"Trust me, I am working on the bringing in of a kingdom, and I have a whole lot of other people in mind besides you and your fatherless child."*[9]

Wow.

I'm writing this book as someone born and raised in America. You might be reading this in Australia, Canada, the United Kingdom, India, or who knows where. What I know about myself is that I was raised to believe that the individual is greater than the group. My "kingdom success"—the building of a life that I believe is best for me—my independence, my story, should be the most important thing to me, and because of that, I expect God to do what's best for *my* kingdom. But as Christians, we represent a different kingdom.

God does do what's best for us, but He does it by doing what's best for His kingdom as a whole. We can always believe He'll do what's best for us, because we know He'll do what's best for Him . . . and what's best for Him is what's best for us. When we say yes to Christ, we lay down the right to our own personal kingdom and give our lives over to His. God doesn't begrudge us asking for what we want or need, but the correct posture for prayer is always just like that of Jesus before He was crucified: "Not my will, but yours, be done" (Luke 22:42). As

Elisabeth Elliot said, "It has been my experience many times, when I pray, 'Thy will be done,' it involves the undoing of my will."[10]

It's unreasonable to think that just because God doesn't answer our prayers the way we want Him to He isn't hearing them. He is. Always. He just might not be giving us the answer we want because it isn't part of His bigger plan. We hold on tightly to our tiny kingdoms with our tiny fists raised to God in defiance and hurt, not realizing that His kingdom is so much bigger than anything we can see or taste or touch or feel. We are a *part* of the kingdom, not the whole thing. We rail against God for letting us hurt when He allowed His own Son to be beaten beyond recognition for our salvation. Says Elliot, "God has never done anything to me that wasn't *for* me."[11] This is the correct perspective, although it doesn't come easily or naturally to most, including me.

It is those who choose to see the events of their lives this way—good or bad—who are able to be fully used for the glory of God. The question is not really *Why doesn't God hear my prayers?* but *What do I believe about my place in God's plan?* Your answer will change how you see everything. Now, let's hear the rest of Gina's story.

At times I have wondered if God hears my prayers or if He even sees what is happening. I have not really known how to pray. It's hard to admit that I sometimes reach a point where I feel too tired to take one more step. But all the voices that whisper in my ear telling me I should have had it all together by age fifty-seven—and that make me feel guilty for having these emotions—are not the voice of truth. Rather than fall into condemnation because I feel these emotions, have questions, or feel alone, God has been teaching me that He wants me to share every single one of them with Him.

God has shown me examples of people in His Word who were facing hopelessness yet still cried out to Him for deliverance. This helps me remember that it's okay to be honest and ask the hard questions as long as I am finding the answers to my challenges in God himself.

It's so comforting and encouraging to know that it's okay to ask questions like . . .

Why?

Where are you, God?

Why can't I hear you, God?

Do you hear my prayers?

How long will this last?

. . . as long as I'm pouring out my heart to Him and choosing to remember the truth of His character and all He's done in the past. This is the choice I have to make one day at a time—sometimes even minute by minute. And then, after God has reminded me of His faithfulness, He challenges me to cling to the hope that is found in Him alone.

As a mom, a wife, a daughter of elderly parents, a friend, and a church member, I can take the difficult, seemingly overwhelming circumstances (and emotions!) that enter each of these parts of my life and lay them all out before God. I can be honest with how I feel about each circumstance, and then I find my hope in Him. He has been faithful all these years, and He will continue to be faithful!

Are you facing some difficult circumstances that have left you feeling hopeless, wondering if God hears your prayers? I can assure you that He does hear them! Let me encourage you with the following verses:

> Blessed are those whose strength is in you, whose hearts are set on pilgrimage. As they pass through the Valley of Baka [Valley of Weeping or

Valley of Tears!], they make it a place of springs; the autumn rains also cover it with pools. They go from strength to strength, till each appears before God in Zion.

Psalm 84:5–7 NIV

Pray It Forward

» Even when you face times of sorrow, loss, grief, and confusion—valleys of weeping—God will provide, even in these sorrows, springs of grace upon grace!

» Choose to go to God in your uncertain and difficult days, knowing that He does hear your prayers and He can handle all that you bring Him.

» God is more than happy when you heap your burdens on His strong shoulders, and when you do this, you can fully focus on, trust in, and find your hope in Him. And He will turn these difficulties into reasons to praise and worship Him!

Prayers

Verse: "As the deer pants for streams of water, so my soul pants for you, my God. My soul thirsts for God, for the living God. When can I go and meet with God? My tears have been my food day and night. . . . Why, my soul, are you downcast? Why so disturbed within me? Put your hope in God, for I will yet praise him, my Savior and my God" (Psalm 42:1–3, 5 NIV).

Prayer: Father, no matter what's happening in my life, help me to put my hope in you and your Word. Even when I feel I can't take one more step, propel me toward the truth of your Word. May I thirst for it always.

Verse: "I waited patiently for the LORD; he turned to me and heard my cry. He lifted me out of the slimy pit, out of the mud and mire; he set my feet on a rock and gave me a firm place to stand. He put a new song in my mouth, a hymn of praise to our God. Many will see and fear the LORD and put their trust in him" (Psalm 40:1–3 NIV).

Prayer: Lord, help me to wait on you. Give me the ability to trust that you'll always come. As I submit my life to you, no matter what, may others be inspired to follow you.

Verse: "You hem me in behind and before, and you lay your hand upon me. . . . If I say, 'Surely the darkness will hide me and the light become night around me,' even the darkness will not be dark to you; the night will shine like the day, for darkness is as light to you'" (Psalm 139:5, 11–12 NIV).

Prayer: Jesus, you are the Light of the World. Shine and show me where to go, and help me to trust that as I follow you, I'm protected within your will.

5

I Can't Pray until I Get My Life Together

Lord, Put Me Back Together

I raced down the highway in our GMC Envoy trying desperately not to be late for the soccer games . . . again. It had become something of a joke—one I wasn't pleased to have attached to our family. But with two little boys and a husband who worked shift work (leaving me as a single mom a lot of the time), I just couldn't seem to get my act together to get anywhere on time.

This particular Saturday morning I just knew we were going to make it. Granted, there was only going to be time enough to kick the boys out the door, go find parking, and get back in time to watch the beginning of the game. But for once, we were going to be on time! I pulled into the parking lot only to find myself the lone car there. My mind exploded. *Where is everyone else? Are we early?*

Then, as if on cue, I received a text from my friend Jamie: "The game is starting!" And I knew. I had messed up again. Frantically, I replied, "Where are you? I'm here alone, and I can't find anyone?" Her reply? "Where are you? Everyone is here." Reality washed over me, reddening my face and neck and making my heart beat faster. I had gone to the wrong field. And the right field? It was over fifteen minutes away. For a game that would last about thirty minutes, it almost wasn't worth it.

I broke the news to my boys, and watched their disappointment in me hit hard . . . again. No matter what I did, I couldn't keep up with our schedule. In fact, the harder I tried, the worse it seemed to get. I had calendars, alarms, emails, and everything else designed to help me remember, but even when I did manage to remember, like that Saturday's game, I mixed up the details. I was a failure, and I didn't know how to fix it. I think that was the worst part. As a girl who had always been able to excel with hard work, I couldn't make the necessary changes, even on behalf of the people I most wanted to please. I struggled on for many months under the weight of guilt, thinking I should be able to figure it out on my own, never asking God to intervene, because I didn't think He should have to. Maybe you can relate?

Moms like you and me who view their lives as messy, disorganized, and maybe even sinful, feel they can't pray and talk to God until they reach a state of being "put together," whatever that looks like for them. We, as a culture, don't think we're supposed to need God for everyday things like getting to a soccer game on time or dealing with temper tantrums, but we need God so much more than we understand. Thankfully, God used motherhood to show me exactly that.

My friend Connie Albers understands what it is to feel like she should be able to figure things out on her own before asking God for help. Let's listen to her story now.

When I was a young mom, I struggled to measure up to the ideal Christian mother. I couldn't make my schedule work. I got impatient. I didn't know how to love unconditionally. Of all the expectations I placed on myself, not being perfect was the most difficult for me. It's odd to admit, but I didn't see myself as a perfectionist until I became a mom. Up to that point, I thought I was an achiever type. When we started having children, I realized how much pressure I put on myself to have it all together. Every day I strived to make it better. I reasoned it had to be better or God wouldn't bless my family.

How could I ask God to bring order to my home if my life wasn't in perfect order? How could I ask the Lord to answer any of my prayers if I wasn't doing my part? All my striving left me worn down and discouraged.

I listened to other moms speak about the power of prayer, but I felt like many of my prayers fell on deaf ears. My upbringing made it difficult for me to believe God answers ordinary prayers. My teen years made me think that I was too broken for God to even listen to me. Unfortunately, that was not a good combination going into marriage or motherhood. The thought that I had to achieve some benchmark before God would hear my requests troubled me. How could my prayers be effective? I often pondered James 5:16, which says, "The effective, fervent prayer of a righteous man avails much" (NKJV), and reasoned that if God heard the righteous prayers, and my prayers weren't being answered, I must not be righteous. That is a challenging problem for any mom.

If anyone in Christian history had a story that should have kept him separated from God, it was the apostle Paul. In his words, he was "formerly a blasphemer, a persecutor, and an arrogant man . . . the worst of [the sinners] . . ." (1 Timothy 1:13, 15). Paul, previously named Saul, knew who he had been, and just how much of God's wrath he deserved. He did not have it all together, from a biblical, Christian perspective, before he met Jesus. In fact, the Scriptures tell us Paul had made it his mission to kill as many Christians as possible. Acts 7:58 tells us that when the first Christian was martyred, Paul was there. Stephen was stoned to death for sharing about Jesus, and Paul watched it happen. When Paul did come to Christ, suddenly and radically (Acts 9), the other believers were afraid of him (9:26), such a violent man—especially toward Christians. Rather than welcoming him into their lives, they had to hear from another person they trusted—Barnabas—that Paul was truly a changed man before they could believe it.

Certainly, most moms reading this chapter don't have a history like Paul's, but in those moments like what I described at the beginning of the chapter—when you've let your loved ones down yet again, or when you've committed that besetting sin again . . . the one you've been trying to overcome for years—it can feel like it. Paul may have been "the worst of sinners," but we moms excel at heaping guilt on ourselves until it feels like we top him.

At a crisis pregnancy center, I once served a mom who was pregnant and addicted to drugs. She desperately wanted to get her life straightened out so that she could provide her child with a good, stable home. She knew about God, and we made slow progress in helping her take steps toward wholeness and healing, helping her get the resources she needed both as a mom and as someone who needed addiction treatment. I encouraged her multiple times throughout our time together to give her life to God and let Him take over. I knew that for her to truly get the help she needed, it was going to take a miracle the size only God can provide, but as far as I know, she never did. She wanted to get her life together before she came to God.

Tragically, she overdosed and died. I was broken and shocked when we found out. She is one of those precious women who have left a mark on my soul. I couldn't reach her, and I so wish we could do it over with different results. She could have given her heart and life to Jesus any time, but she was hindered by her circumstances and her pride. She was tragically misled by the false belief that there was some kind of work to do on her part before she could be acceptable to God. But the truth is, work never makes us acceptable. Our acceptance by God is based on what's in our hearts.

If ever there was someone who didn't have his priorities straight, it was our Paul. And yet, God took control of him (quite literally, read the story of Paul's salvation in Acts 9) and made him into the man he wanted to be after Paul submitted his will and his life to Jesus. God actually used the things about Paul's past that made him feel unworthy to get the most glory out of Paul's life.

So, what needs to be true of us—our character, our values, our habits, our decisions—before we can come to God in prayer? I believe there are just three things, and we'll explore them in this chapter. They include:

1. A desolate position of the heart
2. A belief in God and Jesus, His Son
3. A willingness to ask

A Desolate Position of the Heart

In AD 412, Bishop Augustine, one of the most notable, foundational teachers of the early Christian church, wrote a letter on the topic of prayer to a widow named Proba who was concerned she wasn't praying in the right way. Proba's family was very well-known and well-off in their Roman home, and even though an invasion by a Gothic army forced her to flee and find safety in Africa, Proba continued to serve the Lord alongside her daughter and grand-niece for, as far as we know, the rest of her life. Proba, a personal friend of Augustine (man, what a gift!), asked him to teach her how to pray. He responded by telling her what kind of person she should be in order to have effective prayers. Let me repeat that for the sake of emphasis. Proba asked Augustine to teach her how to pray. Augustine told her *who she needed to be.*

It's notable, at least to me as a woman, that Augustine, in a time when women were not valued—their opinions worthless—took the time to respond to her at all. In his return letter to her, easily accessible now to us on the internet, he says some profound things, but this quote is my favorite. When asked how to pray, he replied, "You must account yourself 'desolate' in this world, however great the prosperity of your lot may be."[1]

As far as we know, Proba's family was very wealthy. There's nothing in her story that suggests she lost all of that wealth, or even her status when she fled Rome, so her desolation, meaning a sad or wretched condition, didn't come from her physical or material well-being. No, the desolation Augustine is referring to here is a condition on the inside of the person—the condition of the heart.

You see, God doesn't expect us to have it all together before we come to Him. I'd like to suggest to you that the time when we most need help, when we feel we are at our worst, is the time we can see His provision and grab hold of it most clearly. There is no one who comes to Christ who doesn't first have the solid, fully formed thought, *I am a sinner*. But that's not the only sure thought she has. No, it's followed closely by a second thought, as surely as if she found herself struggling to stay above water to keep from drowning after falling out of a boat: *I need a Savior*. It is only when we see our great need—all the things we can't fix by ourselves—that we know we need help. And what is prayer, after all, but asking God for His divine help? It isn't just that we need to let go of the idea that we have to have it all together. We need to actively reject it. My client freely admitted she was a sinner, but she couldn't admit she needed a Savior.

The Christian life is not waiting around until everything is perfect, or until we're able to *make* everything perfect. It's seeing the fullness of our wretched condition—our desolation—apart from God, realizing He's the only one who *can* fix it, and running to Him to get the kind of help only He can give. And when I say run, what I really mean is dive head and heart first into His amazing grace.

Let's look to the Word of God to explain this to us in more depth. Consider with me the verses that, when I read them for the first time—*really* read them—overwhelmed me for days:

> For while we were still helpless, at the right time, Christ died for the ungodly. For rarely will someone die for a just person—though for a good person perhaps someone might even dare to die. But God proves his own love for us in that while we were still sinners, Christ died for us.
>
> Romans 5:6–8

Catch the language used above: "helpless," "ungodly," "still sinners." What is there to indicate in these verses that we must clean ourselves up before coming to God? Nothing. And to seal the deal, lest we still have a nagging suspicion that we have to have it all together *ever*, there's Colossians 1:17, which says, "He is before all things, and by him all things hold together." No, we're not the ones who hold it all together. God is, and we don't have to be perfect or cleaned up before coming to Him. He wants us to come as we are. He'll do the cleaning up as we grow to know and love Him more.

I believe our desire to "make things right" in our lives before coming to God comes from a position of pride and a desire not to lose control of our lives. We want to be the ones to get things sorted out because we want to believe we can, but we can't. This desire—to maintain control—is an illusion, because we aren't in control in any way. Paul Miller, in one of my favorite books on prayer, *A Praying Life*, says this:

> What do I lose when I have a praying life? Control. Independence. What do I gain? Friendship with God. A quiet heart. The living work of God in the hearts of those I love. The ability to roll back the tide of evil. Essentially, I lose my kingdom and get his. I move from being an independent player to a dependent lover. I move from being an orphan to a child of God.[2]

We want to keep what we believe to be our own power, our own autonomy, when in reality, the true power comes in letting it go.

Let it go.

A Belief in God and Jesus, His Son

In so many ways, prayer represents the heart of the gospel. I see that I am sinful, helpless to save myself, and desperate for

God to intervene. I ask, He freely gives. That's the gospel in a nutshell. It's also what happens when we pray.

The most important step to having a vibrant prayer life is believing in God and Jesus, His Son. In his book *Desiring God*, John Piper says, "Prayer is the open admission that without Christ we can do nothing. And prayer is the turning away from ourselves to God in the confidence that He will provide the help we need. Prayer humbles us as needy and exalts God as wealthy."[3]

Do you really believe that? That without Christ you can do nothing? Oh sure, you can do some things, but I wonder if you've ever reached the point in your life where there was something you couldn't do . . . something that tripped you up? Made you desperate? The fact that you picked up this book is an indicator that maybe you have, and that at least on some level you know Jesus is the answer. But if you haven't, you will, and I've learned that it's God's kindness to us to let it happen as early in life as possible, to let us dig and dig and try and try until we realize we need Him. This is what belief in God and Jesus means. Not just an intellectual nod to their existence. Not even just knowing you need Jesus for salvation. But belief that you need Jesus each and every moment of every day.

Do you believe the promises of God are true?

Do you believe they're true for you?

Do you believe God is in control of even the hardest moments of your life?

Do you believe His plans for you are good? Even the ones that feel bad?

Do you believe God's Word is true, and that your life should be a reflection of what's inside?

Do you believe that God will meet all your needs according to His riches in Christ Jesus?

Do you believe He's there with you when the kids are crazy and you can't fix it?

Do you believe God can pick up the pieces of your broken life and make something beautiful from it?

This kind of belief is what we need more of in the hearts of moms like us, because it's this kind of belief that puts God in His proper place on the throne of our hearts and empowers our prayers to be used of God to further His kingdom.

A Willingness to Ask

A few nights ago, my husband came home to find me at the tail end of a bad day. I don't remember now why it was so bad, but I'm sure it had something to do with an overloaded schedule, unmet expectations, and no idea what we were having for dinner. As I walked out the door to take one of our sons to his practice and pick the other up from the high school, he asked what the dinner plan was. In a huff, I threw up my hands and fussed, "I have no idea! I'm juggling all the things, and I can't juggle dinner too!" I think he knew I was sincere, even if my tone was a little fussy. I really had been stressed lately, as had he, and he wanted to help. By the time I got back from running all the boys around to all the places, he had dinner on the table. Granted, it was fried hot dogs and potatoes (his specialty), but it was dinner. When I thanked him, he said, "All you had to do was ask."

Sometimes the answer is just too easy.

Psalm 116:2, one of my favorite verses, tells us that God bends down to listen to us. He isn't off in heaven too busy or distracted to know what's happening in our lives. He hasn't forgotten about us, and He isn't worried about our futures. According to this Scripture, the posture of God's ear is bent toward us. In fact, the full verse says, "Because he bends down to listen, I will pray as long as I have breath!" (NLT). It's knowing that God is listening and waiting for us to admit our need for Him that gives me the faith to ask, and keep asking.

If you struggle with feeling like you have to fix everything before you can pray, take a moment to reflect on Psalm 116:2. God is waiting for you to ask, and His plans for you are good.

Truly, the only three things required to come before God are a desolate heart, belief in God and His Son, Jesus, and a willingness to ask. It's a matter of the state of your heart, not the state of your life. I spent entirely too much time fumbling around in the dark trying to be super mom just because I thought I should be able to fix my own problems, make my children behave, and arrive at places on time. The reality was that I couldn't. My very best efforts fell short over and over, and even when things looked good on the outside, they often weren't on the inside, where it counts. I'm not trying to say our home was a total failure. It wasn't. But if I had laid my pride aside earlier and admitted to God I needed His help, it would've saved me a lot of heartache. My heart was right with God as it related to my salvation, but it took the mess of motherhood to help me see how much I needed Him every day.

Lay your pride aside.

You can go to God now, right where you are, and tell Him you need help. That you need to work on your own to put things back together is a lie meant to keep you from God, and with God—relying on His strength instead of your own—is where the miracles happen.

Consider praying this prayer (and hear the voices of many other Christians along with you):*

Father, I need you. Not just for this one moment, but for every moment of my life to come. Teach me what it means to lay my burdens down at your feet and not pick them up again. I confess, Lord, I don't always know what it looks like to live a true Christian life, and I'm a little bit scared to let go of control and give you permission to fix me instead of trying to fix myself, but I hear you calling me to trust you, so I'm asking you to be true to your Word and meet me right where I am with grace and a clear path forward. Please help me trust you with the things that might be holding me back so that I can walk with you for the rest of my life. In Jesus' name, amen.

Now let's hear the rest of Connie's story.

• • ❋ • •

My struggle drove me to search God's Word for answers. I read many examples of God answering the prayers of women . . . women like me asking for the same thing—wisdom, discernment, direction, and other things—and God used a verse in Scripture to teach me an important truth. I read Romans 3:10, which says, "There is none righteous, no, not one" (NKJV), and thought, *If there is no one righteous, yet He hears the righteous prayers, how does that work?* This verse, combined with my deeper study, showed me I didn't have to have it all together to go before the Lord in prayer. We are righteous because of our position in Christ.

*If you have never made the decision to follow Jesus, please take a moment right now and visit appendix 2 at the back of this book. I'll walk you through it.

God doesn't wait for us to become righteous before we can pray. I learned that a righteous person isn't the standard; righteousness is a process of learning to obey His commands, surrendering to His will, and continually learning to trust God in all things. God taught me how He uses our faith in Him to restore, heal, lead, and guide us. God's silence isn't necessarily an indicator that He's waiting on us to get it all together. Many times, waiting for God's answer to my prayers has been His protection for me. The moment we start to believe we have to have it all together before we pray is the instant we most need to pray.

God doesn't look for perfection, not from me or you. He wants us to seek Him, to be faithful, and to trust Him to lead us in raising our children.

Pray It Forward

» Begin every morning with prayer. Before my feet hit the floor, I ask the Lord to equip me for today's assignment. Your confidence will increase when you start your day with Him.

» Consistently cast your cares on the Lord and trust Him to work all things out according to His plan for your life and family.

» Ask for wisdom to discern your thoughts so you aren't discouraged by the enemy. When you start to doubt your ability to pray, remember this important truth: Believe God wants to hear your prayers; believe He isn't waiting until you reach a certain standard before you pray; and allow God to grow your faith in Him through your prayers.

- » Many moms struggle with discouragement and anger. Some moms wrestle with trusting God to answer their prayers if they don't have it all together. If you've felt discouragement, anger, or lack of trust, may I encourage you to take hold of those thoughts? Your prayers matter to God.
- » God doesn't expect us to have it all together. God is at work. He is faithful; He isn't silent.

Prayers

Verse: "Give instruction to a wise man, and he will be still wiser; teach a righteous man, and he will increase in learning" (Proverbs 9:9 ESV).

Prayer: Father, make my heart wise so that I can learn to be even wiser. Move me forward in growing to be more like your Son so that I can increase in learning.

Verse: "Cast your burden on the LORD, and he will sustain you; he will never permit the righteous to be moved" (Psalm 55:22 ESV).

Prayer: Lord, so often I try to hold on to my own burdens. When I do, I miss out on the freedom you've offered me in your ability to carry them for me. Sustain me as I trust you through my hardest times.

Verse: "Blessed are those who hunger and thirst for righteousness, for they shall be filled" (Matthew 5:6 NKJV).

Prayer: Lord, give me a hunger and thirst for your Word, and to follow you.

Verse: "And be found in Him, not having my own righteousness, which is from the law, but that which is through faith in Christ, the righteousness which is from God by faith" (Philippians 3:9 NKJV).

Prayer: Lord, help me not to be derailed when I fall short, but instead, trust that I'm covered by the righteousness of Christ. His righteousness covers all my failures today and every day.

I Have Small Children. I Can't Even Think, Much Less Pray!

Lord, Teach Me to Pray in the Moments of My Day

Here's where the rubber meets the road.

We've spent a lot of time in this book so far addressing issues of the heart that prevent us from being the kind of praying moms we want to be, and now it's time to get practical. Every time I share about the impact prayer has had on my life, I get the same question from moms of young children: "I have small children. I can't even think, much less pray! How in the world can I still be a praying mom?" They want practical tips for incorporating prayer into the craziness of the early years, and I'm going to give those in this chapter and the next, but it's been my experience—especially as a mom now of teenagers—that it never gets easier to create space for this vital piece of our walk with God. It just doesn't. The challenges and issues might look different across the ages and stages, but there will always be obstacles to creating time to do the most important thing. I promise. Don't put it off until later, thinking you'll have more time. I'm just as tired and worn-out now as I was when mine were little. It's just from different things.

Ruth Bell Graham said, "Satan fears prayer because God hears prayer."[1] If you're a mom of young children whose brain feels like mush most days, and who goes to bed each night wondering if you can possibly have the strength to get up the next day and do it all over again, you need to be praying. I'm not telling you that to heap guilt on you, or to make you feel like you have to somehow make time for one more thing. I'm just telling you that praying God's Word is the most important thing—the *only* thing that helped me see straight when I was in that stage of mothering—and it continues to be the only thing to this day. Let's hear from my friend Suzanne Gosselin, author and mother of four, on this subject. She gets it.

I hit a spiritual slump around the time my third child turned one. With three children five years and under, including one with special needs, the sheer number of daily tasks began to crowd out any and all alone time I could have with the Lord. From the moment I woke up in the morning to when I closed my eyes at night, I was going, going, going . . . caring for my little ones and my husband.

Before I had children, I worked at a Christian organization for ten years and was accustomed to having copious amounts of time for prayer. I loved to pray out loud in my car on my way to and from work or other places. I got together with a girlfriend once a week to pray for specific things we were going through. I prayed each morning and before bed.

When I had my first child, and eventually three more during the following six years, those discretionary moments of prayer began to fade away. I was *always* busy changing diapers, preparing food, washing sticky faces, cleaning up messes, reading picture books, or making peace between warring siblings. Even though I knew my family was a blessing, many days I felt much more stressed than blessed.

One day it occurred to me that I was running on spiritual fumes. Our family attended church each Sunday, but during the week, I rarely spent time in prayer. With so much on my plate, I felt like I didn't have the bandwidth to even think of the words to say in those precious moments when I could find the time. This lack of prayer was not only affecting my relationship with the Lord, it was also impacting my ability to be a good mom. When frustrations arose (and they did daily—and even hourly most days), I would erupt in anger. When I felt so needy myself, I struggled to lovingly address the needs of my children. I could clearly see I wasn't living out the fruit of the Spirit, which includes joy, peace, patience, and gentleness (Galatians 5:22–23). Instead of thriving in the God-given role of motherhood, I was stuck in survival mode.

I have to tell you, I can totally relate to Suzanne's story. My prayer and Bible study life came to a screeching halt when I stopped working in full-time ministry too. For about ten years, including the time before I was married and had children, I worked in crisis pregnancy ministries across the state of Virginia, and one of the hallmarks of these amazing ministries is that they run quite literally on prayer. Prayer for the finances to provide services, prayer for salvation, prayer for their clients as they make life-and-death decisions, prayer for the needs of volunteers and staff, prayer for the community. Every single day I served in these centers of respite for women in unplanned pregnancy, I sat down for a time of dedicated prayer at least three times as different shifts of volunteers came in. I think my prayer life grew and developed there in ways that prepared me to turn back to it when I was in crisis in my own motherhood, but when I stepped down to be at home full-time with my boys (they were five and three at the time), I lost that connection with other very mature men and women who loved the Lord, and I sincerely missed it.

It's hard to stay connected to God when you're not connected to a family of believers. Of course, we attended church regularly, and we attended home groups as we were able with young children, but I always felt that those young children kept us from being able to participate in the way I wanted to. Because of the nature of my husband's job, he only gets one or two Sundays a month in church with us, so I was left wrestling the boys when he wasn't there—and wrestling them when he was. Not because he didn't want to help (he always did), but because I wanted him to be free to get as much as he could out of the one or two Sundays he had with our church family. It was a never-ending cycle—one that found me sneaking out the back doors of the church most Sundays before communion so I wouldn't have to wrangle them to the front of the church. In that season, it just felt like there was no quiet place, no harbor of peace *anywhere*, that would allow me to hear from God.

There were so many wonderful things about that time of our lives that I look back on now with joy and laughter. I remember fondly, and a little longingly, the days when my boys wore capes everywhere we went. I love to think about my youngest's brutal overbite that caused him to have a pronounced (and adorable) lisp when he was little (it's gone now). I remember how everything was an adventure to them, how they loved sports even when they were tiny, and how I had different spots where I would kiss them good-night (and if I messed it up and kissed the wrong boy on the forehead or on the nose, they would call me out on it!). I remember their soft, wispy hair, the way my oldest sucked his thumb on one hand and kept his other tangled in my hair, and I remember dancing them to sleep as infants, thinking I just couldn't imagine a time when we didn't feel this close. (I'm not crying, *you're* crying!) Thankfully, my husband and I worked hard to try to maintain a close relationship with our kids, but I'm here to tell you that it does change. It should.

While I remember those precious times of their early childhood with joy and tenderness now, the sheer physicality, the sweatiness, the tears, and the frustrations that came with these things colored most of my experience of their little years so that I'm not sure I enjoyed them as much as I could have, and that makes me sad. Please believe me when I tell you that turning to God, and learning to pray His Word, is what kept me sane in one of the hardest seasons of my life. I've written before about having hard-to-handle boys. In fact, I wrote a whole program about learning to fight FOR them instead of AGAINST them, and how this changed everything for me. But the most important part of learning to fight for them was learning to fight for them in prayer. What I meant to be something that changed them changed me. I don't want to think about where we'd be if God hadn't led me to that place.

So let's dive in and figure out how to make it work.

As the first part of our practical guide to prayer, I want to lay some ground rules. Nothing legalistic . . . just some rules for prayer written by noted theologian John Calvin that can serve as our guide or a reminder about the importance of the posture of our hearts before we start.

Five Rules for Prayer

Found in his work *Institutes of the Christian Religion* are Calvin's five rules for prayer. Using Tim Keller's book *Prayer* as a foundation, I'm going to paraphrase them here and try to translate them into mom language so we can all understand (because frankly, sometimes these older, incredibly wise theologians talk right over my head).

Why is this important to do first? Because God sees your heart, sweet mom of littles. He knows you need Him. He sees you in all your tired, worn-out, weary glory, and He knows that motherhood will stretch your heart, strain it, and cause you to question things about your faith that you never questioned before. Although motherhood is a tool God uses to make us more like Him, it tends to make our hearts and emotions run amok. Personally, motherhood made me question God like never before. But I'm glad it did, because it forced me to make peace with aspects of God's character and how He grows His kingdom that I might never have grappled with apart from it. That's what I want to do in this section: give you the tools to settle some of the most important things about God in your heart as you prepare to pray and help you understand why they're important for you as a mom.

Rule #1: Fear God

John Piper says, "Jesus calls us to pray first and foremost for his name to be hallowed, his Kingdom to come, his will to be done."[2] What, though, does it mean for God's name to be "hallowed"? What does it mean to fear God?

In chapter 4 I told you about an experience I had while attending a blogging conference. Now, to demonstrate the idea of fearing God, I want to tell you something else that happened to me at that same conference. I got in on the blogging scene a few years after it exploded, and when I started sharing and teaching online, there were already a few spiritual giants on the scene who were leading the way for those of us coming behind them. One was Ann Voskamp, the author of *One Thousand Gifts: A Dare to Live Fully Right Where You Are*. Ann is a self-professed introvert with a lovely gift for writing. Her prose is easy to spot, and in the beginning, watching another introvert scratch out words here and there in between living on a farm and taking care of her family seemed too good to be true. It was so close to my dream. I loved Ann. I loved the way she made God's Word come alive through everyday events. I loved the way she and her husband lived a simple but God-glorifying life. I loved her shy awkwardness. I even loved the way she read her notes when she spoke in public. I loved watching God grow her and shape her into something she may never have dreamed she would become.

And so when I got the chance to meet Ann at this blogging conference after her life-changing keynote session, I was a little awestruck. Okay, a lot. And I wasn't the only one. I didn't want to stand in the long line of women waiting to meet her, so I just hung back in a corner of the room until she was almost finished, and then stepped into the back of the line. When I approached her, she immediately grabbed my hands and said, "Brooke! I've been wanting to meet you! Thank you for leading us in how to pray for our boys. Your work is so valuable." I have no idea what I said back to her. It probably included a heartfelt thank-you for the work she was doing that was impacting me and so many, but honestly, I was just stunned that she even knew my name, much less what I wrote about most often.

I don't mean to make an idol of Ann Voskamp. She's not God, but I was drawn to God in her. She represented someone I admired and whose words impacted my life in a profound way (as she did for so many), and I was a little bit in awe of being with her. There were other speakers there that weekend who shared important words. They were valuable, but Ann was the one I really wanted to meet.

So it is with God. Fearing Him is being in awe of who He is and loving Him for what He's done with such depth that it binds you, drives you to seek Him out. It's knowing that HE is the One you need to meet, no matter what—no matter how long you have to wait, or what hoops you must jump through to get to Him. Regardless of whether you find Him singing praises in the shower, or hiding in the bathroom, or during that rare afternoon nap time, your mission is clear: Get to God, and don't let anything stand in your way. Not even the beautiful mess of motherhood, and all its responsibilities and distractions, should keep us from the One who knows our name.

Practical tip: What if you've realized that your fear of God is small, or clearly still has room to grow? What if you don't place more value on God than on anything else, even those precious little ones? At least not naturally? What if you don't have an awe of God that makes you want to do whatever it takes to get to Him? That's okay! In fact, it's great that you see it. It is a good gift from your Father to show you something you haven't seen before about your relationship with Him. And there's a solution. (Hint? It's prayer!) Right now, wherever you are, ask God to show you His majesty. Ask Him sincerely to wow you anew with who He is, and to give you a fresh understanding of His role and provisions in your life.

He knows your name. Allow yourself to be blown away by it! It can sound something like this:

> *Father, I want to know you more than I do now. I confess that I'm tired and worn-out and often find it difficult to want to do anything at all. I need to be reminded of how big and strong and mighty you are. Let me feel deeply and see clearly your hand of provision for me now and in the days to come, and may that knowledge make me want to do whatever it takes to get to you. In Jesus' name.*

Rule #2: Know You Need God

In the Western world, it's difficult to see how much we need God. We have so much and are able to get so many things for ourselves, including the bread we eat and the water we drink. I have never, not for one day, lived in fear of not having food or clean water. In fact, I keep little bottles of cold, clean water in the fridge in our garage for the neighborhood kids who constantly occupy our backyard on hot days. I don't have serious material needs, but *nothing* has shown me the depth of my spiritual needs like motherhood. In *Gospel-Centered Mom*, I described it like this:

> Chuck Swindoll says, "Our problem isn't that we've failed. Our problem is that we haven't failed enough. We haven't been brought low enough to learn what God wants us to learn." That was my problem. Before age twenty-seven, when I gave birth to our first son, I had experienced challenges but had always been able to overcome them with hard work and determination. . . . I worked hard at the things I wanted in life, and I was almost always able to achieve them . . . and then I had babies. God used motherhood to take me down a notch or two (or fifty).[3]

I think it might be accurate to say that I never really knew how much I needed God until I had children. I knew I needed Christ for salvation—I settled that in my childhood—but I had no working concept of what it meant to need Him every moment of every day. I had always prayed when I felt like I needed an extra boost, like before an exam or when my grandmother was in the hospital, but I had never needed God like I began to need Him when I became a mom.

Confession. I hated needing God at first. I didn't want to need anyone. I had always prided myself on being able to handle whatever life threw my way, and I wanted people to believe I was strong. I *was* strong, until suddenly I wasn't, and that realization, that I didn't have what it took to be the kind of mom I wanted to be to the boys God had given me, shook me to the core. Imagine thinking you know yourself and then suddenly realizing you aren't as amazing as you thought you were. My opinion of myself leading up to motherhood was entirely too high, and God used my children to knock my prideful feet out from under me in all the best ways. He still does.

Looking back, I am 100 percent grateful that God allowed this season of desperation. In the moment, I often asked God why He was letting this happen to me, but now I know the depth of meaning behind Elisabeth Elliot's words, "God has never done anything to me that wasn't *for* me." I had believed that my greatest need was to be able to raise godly men. But God used motherhood to show me that what I actually needed more than anything else is God himself, and that knowledge is what keeps me on my knees in prayer. It was the realization that I cannot possibly raise godly men on my own, even with a loving husband who is a wonderful father, even taking them to church every Sunday, and even with doing our best to teach them about God, speaking of Him "when you sit in your house and when you walk along the road, when you lie down and when you get up" (Deuteronomy 6:7).

God is the One who changes hearts of stone to hearts of flesh (Ezekiel 36:26). We're only partnering with Him in the process.

Practical tip: The very things that make prayer and time in God's Word challenging when we're parenting young children can be used instead to propel us toward Him. Completely legitimate thieves of our time, like changing diapers, wiping noses, preparing meals, bedtime rituals, and all the responsibilities in between, threaten to keep us from Jesus, when in reality they can make us even more aware of our desperation for Him. Next time you find yourself overwhelmed with your list of things to get done for the day, or frustrated by the toddler's twentieth temper tantrum, or exhausted by a lack of sleep, let those emotions serve as indicators that you need God right then in that moment. Don't allow your feelings to keep you from prayer. Instead, use them to train yourself to pray something like this:

> *Lord, please come. You are the God who bends down to listen (Psalm 116:2), so please hear me. Flood me with your peace. Fill me with your truth. Make them real and alive, and make them work in me right now. Give me your strength to deal with this moment in a way that honors and glorifies you. In Jesus' name.*

Rule #3: Want God's Will More Than Your Own

When I was in my early twenties, I started working at my first full-time job. Each morning, before I had to be at work, I snuck off to a local coffee shop that was in the basement of a downtown building in historic Staunton, Virginia. It was such a cool atmosphere for a young twenty-something who wasn't married yet and had no responsibility to anyone except herself. Even my boyfriend (who would later become my husband) lived several hours away. It was really just me. During that time, I studied passages like Proverbs 3:5–6 ("Trust in the LORD with all your heart, and do not rely on your own understanding; in all your ways know him, and he will make your paths straight") and Psalm 37:4 ("Take delight in the LORD, and he will give you your heart's desires"), and began the process of learning what it meant to let the Lord change my dreams and use me in ways I had never even thought of.

And then I got engaged, and my future husband's job forced him to move to a remote part of Virginia, near the Richmond area. I went with his parents to visit one weekend and to help find a place for him to live, and I was floored at what I saw. In a matter of minutes, it was clear to me that I did not want to live there after our wedding. It was absolutely nothing like beautiful, historic Staunton, not even anything like the pretty small town I grew up in. Worse, it was five hours away from our parents. If there's anything we've been accused of that is 100 percent accurate, it's that I'm a daddy's girl and he's a mama's boy. Neither of us liked it, but, as my mama told me on the phone, "Brooke, if you want to marry that boy, that's where you're going to have to go."

One Sunday when I was visiting the area, once again looking for a place to live after we were married, I decided to attend a church service just over the North Carolina line. I walked in to vibrant worship, and felt immediately like I was supposed to be there. I don't know if you've ever had the experience of just knowing a sermon was meant for you, but that day, in a church I randomly picked out of the Yellow Pages phone book (no smartphones or web pages to look at during those days, friends), the sermon was for me.

God met me that morning in a powerful way through the preaching of His Word. The passage was a random one I'd never studied before from the Old Testament. It told the story of a decorated military leader with the misfortune of having leprosy. In the story, a servant girl of Naaman's wife knew about the prophet Elisha and believed Elisha could heal her mistress's husband. So Naaman took off to Israel, loaded down with gold, silver, and clothing, to find his healing, and when our man of honor, highly valued in his own country, arrived at the door to Elisha's home, Elisha sent a messenger to open the door to him and tell him what to do.

Naaman got mad. Insulted. He had come with a display of riches and wealth, in his mind to show honor and deference to Elisha, and what did he get in return? A servant of Elisha's who told him to go dip in a muddy river seven times. Second Kings 5:11 tells us Naaman expected a ceremony fit for his level of importance, where Elisha would "stand and call on the name of the Lord his God, and wave his hand over the place and cure the skin disease." And washing in the muddy Jordan River when there were cleaner, grander rivers in his own home that were more befitting of his station? No, thanks. Had it not been for Naaman's own servants begging him to go and do what the prophet advised, to lower himself and choose God's way of doing things over his own, he would have missed the blessing. "So Naaman went down and dipped himself in the Jordan seven times, according to the command of the man of God. Then his skin was restored and became like the skin of a small boy, and he was clean" (2 Kings 5:14).

I sat in my chair, alone, in the middle of a church full of people I had never met (but would come to love), and experienced a direct answer from God to me. Marrying my husband meant dipping myself in a place I saw a bit like the Jordan River, and if I didn't, I would miss the blessing God had for me.

There have been other muddy rivers God has metaphorically asked me to dip in since that time, but each time I've fought Him on it, wanting my will more than His own. And each time, though not without struggle, heartache, and even loss, His will has been proven to be better than mine. Praying to the God who runs the entire universe and who created you requires the ability, even when it's hard, to actually embrace the answer He gives you. As Elisabeth Elliot said, "How shall I pray 'Thy kingdom come' unless I hold the world to be His to begin with."[4]

Practical tip: My friend Stacey Thacker, whom you've already heard from in this book, once told me, "God isn't doing something to you. He's doing something in you and for you. Maybe even through you." This perspective makes it easier for me to stop demanding my own way. Naaman was insulted by what he was asked to do to be cured, and sometimes we react the same way to what God asks of us—offended when God doesn't do what we think is best. Once again, the answer to this issue is one of prayer. If you see yourself in this story, maybe even as a mom who feels like God has asked her to completely set her own will aside for His (and you're bristling a bit over it), pray like this:

Lord, I don't like the season of life you have me in, and I don't understand why I have to be here. I don't know why you won't make it easier, and my pride is tempting me to take offense at what you're asking me to do. Help me to see things your way. Help me trust you in this moment. Help me to believe you're good and that you're using this time to do something in, for, and maybe even through me. In Jesus' name.

Rule #4: Have Faith Even When You Can't See

I've struggled for years with the sovereignty of God. I believe God is over all and in all and in control of all, yet I also believe He gives us free will. I once heard a pastor explain these two apparently contradictory theologies as being the "twin towers" of Scripture. They're both there: God is in complete control AND we have free will. I will not undertake to explain it any further than that myself, because much more learned men and women than me struggle, but from that solid, yet confusing explanation I take this truth: There are going to be some things I will never understand fully this side of heaven. That's why it's called *faith*.

Hebrews 11 is often referred to as the "Hall of Faith." It is filled with stories of the greats of the Bible, many of whom never saw the fulfillment of what God promised them. Through this passage, we're given great examples of great men and women of God who chose to live in faith even when it cost them something, even when they couldn't see the future, because they wanted to please God.

Abel offered all he had to God in faith and was murdered for it.

Enoch was "taken away" by God and never experienced death because he was a faithful man.

Noah built a massive boat and experienced ridicule from his friends and neighbors out of faith and obedience to God even though there was no rain in the land.

Abraham left his home and didn't even know where God would take him. He continued to live in a foreign land, away from all that he had known, because it served the purpose of God.

Sarah, his wife, lived into her old age waiting for God to fulfill His promise to her of a son, enduring the shame that was then associated with not being able to have children.

Moses's parents hid him instead of allowing him to be killed with the other male children his age, choosing to have faith that God would do something with his life.

Even prostitutes, murderers, slanderers, and liars were given the right to exercise faith by God, and that's very good news for you and me.

God rarely, if ever, gives us glimpses of what will be. Sometimes we don't even get to see why He asked us to do something until after the fact.

The people of Hebrews 11 never got to see the end result of their faith: Jesus. And you and I might live without knowing the purpose of our obedience and suffering. But we can have faith in the God who, from the beginning, has known the end. We can choose to have faith that He's good and that His plans for us are good, even if they don't look or feel good in the moment. Choosing to have faith in God's bigger plan is the substance and heartbeat of a mature prayer life, really, a mature life. We may not always get what we hope for, and we might sometimes (often) be told to wait, but God always does what He says He'll do, and this knowledge gives us hope.

Practical tip: Faith, by definition, is something we can't see. For moms, faith can mean believing our children will eventually sleep through the night, or that they will not start kindergarten in diapers. More often, faith is giving our kids the grace to grow out of and through whatever stage they're currently in. When my boys were little, I often lacked the long-game perspective, meaning I struggled to think anything about the season my kids were currently in would ever change. Of course, now, with two teenagers, I know I was shortsighted, but the challenge of the moment blinded me from hope and kept me from having faith in what God could do. I regret that. I wish I could go back and shake my younger mom self and say, "This too shall pass! Trust God!" God's Word, specifically Hebrews 11, serves as our "firm shake." It reminds us that most of the faith-filled life is hoping in what is unseen, hard to understand, and, often, delayed. When you're going through a difficult season that makes it hard to have hope for tomorrow, or maybe even for the next moment, pray like this:

> *Father, my vision seems blurry. I can't see you clearly. I feel shortsighted and blind and a little bit helpless, but I know you're there. Help me to see beyond this moment. Let me see the sun through the clouds of my circumstances. Shake me and remind me that waiting isn't wrong or bad. Help me to trust in you. In Jesus' name.*

Rule #5: Remember, It's All Because of Grace

I define biblical grace as unmerited favor, unearned love. You can't do anything for it, you can do nothing to get it, and, on your own, you can't keep it. God gives our prayers favor not because of a set of rules we follow, not because we pray Scripture, but because of His Son.

I have always placed great value on earning. I believed I could earn my way to almost anything I wanted in life, and when it came time for me to parent, I approached it the same way. I thought I would earn righteous children by being the perfect mom. You already know the ending to that story. Even now, my children are far from perfect, and as far as I can tell, they (I) will stay imperfect until we're with God in heaven. Because I understand this, I now have a clearer picture of the worth of their growth than I did before. When they grow, when they mature, when they get some deeper spiritual truth for the first time, I know it had nothing to do with anything good about me, and everything to do with the goodness of God.

As a Christian, God looks at you and sees His Son, with whom He is well pleased (Luke 3:22). Your prayers, imperfect and biased as they might be, are heard by God because Jesus is heard by God, and, as a believer, you are covered by, or *in*, Him. So, while you might endeavor to keep all five of these rules (and keep your head in the right place), remember that none of them, not even all of them together at the same time, makes any difference apart from the same grace of God that granted us salvation in the first place. As the late American preacher R. A. Torrey wrote, "We should go to God in our prayers not on the ground of any goodness in ourselves, but on the ground of Jesus Christ's claim."[5]

Now let's hear the rest of Suzanne's story.

When I realized how spiritually depleted I had become, I knew I had to take action. I remembered something I had heard from a colleague many years before. While working in a stressful newspaper office for over twenty years, he would sneak away to the copy room or supply closet for five minutes to pray. He did this daily, multiple times a day, praying constantly, as the apostle Paul advocated in 1 Thessalonians 5:17. He described how this small act of constantly rededicating his day to Christ had led to many amazing opportunities to share his faith with co-workers and stay strong in a godless environment.

As I thought about his example, I wondered if I could implement something similar into my daily routine. I started by using my time in the car while dropping my son off at preschool, as five-minute moments to pray. At first, my prayers were very simple and focused on getting through that day. But sometimes a friend's request or a family matter would come to mind, and I'd pray for that too.

As my children grew older, I would involve them in prayer. "Hey, guys," I would say, "Daddy has an important meeting today. Who wants to pray for him?" Or, "Remember how we were talking about Pastor Jeff, who has cancer? Let's pray that God will heal his body." Not only did these prayer breaks help me reconnect with God throughout my day, but they also modeled to my children how we can approach the throne of grace with confidence at any hour of the day (Hebrews 4:16).

Praying in the car became part of our family culture. It also became a daily lifeline of connection between me and God. As I talked to him throughout my day, I was reminded of the amazing resource I have as a mom through my relationship with Jesus. No matter what I'm facing or how sleep deprived I am, I can do all things through Him who gives me strength (Philippians 4:13). That's not just a warm, fuzzy thought to stitch on a pillow. God offers real power, strength, and help when I reach out to Him throughout my day.

Pray It Forward

- A lot of moms struggle to adapt their spiritual walk to the demands of being a busy (and stressed-out) mom. Give yourself grace; do even just one small thing for your spiritual life every day.
- Lower your expectations, especially if you had vibrant times in prayer and God's Word before you had kids. Realize in this season your spiritual life will look different than it has in the past (and will in the future).

- » Seek out community with other Christian moms, even (or especially) if you're an introvert. You need to be encouraged and have the peace that comes from knowing you're not alone.
- » Let go of the guilt and shame. Remember that God is gentle with you, understands your limitations, and offers you help and hope in your weakness.

Prayers

Verse: "Come to me, all of you who are weary and burdened, and I will give you rest" (Matthew 11:28).

Prayer: Lord, I need rest. Not just the kind of rest that a day at the spa brings, no. I need rest for my soul. I know that no cup of coffee, no fresh mani/pedi, not even a good night's sleep can bring me that kind of rest. It only comes from you. So here I am. Please refresh my soul in your Word. Open it up to me with the time I have and make it enough.

Verse: "He tends his flock like a shepherd: He gathers the lambs in his arms and carries them close to his heart; he gently leads those that have young" (Isaiah 40:11 NIV).

Prayer: Father, help me to remember your promise to gently lead me. Your heart is so tender toward me as I raise my little ones. I so long for them to know you and follow you. Help me to get the strength I need from your Word each day so that I'll have something of you to pass on to them.

Verse: "But he said to me, 'My grace is sufficient for you, for my power is perfected in weakness.' Therefore, I will most gladly boast all the more about my weaknesses, so that Christ's power may reside in me" (2 Corinthians 12:9).

Prayer: Lord, I'm weak. I don't feel like I have much to bring to the table, but that's okay. Your Word says your grace is enough for me, and that your power is made perfect in my weaknesses . . . so here I am, Lord, all my weaknesses laid out for you to see. Be perfect in me. Let your power dwell in me.

7

I'm So Busy!

Lord, Help Me Find Time for My Most Important Relationship

I can't think of very many women who are busier than my friend September McCarthy. She is a mom of ten, grandmother to nine, as well as an author, podcaster, and conference host. But don't let all of those titles make you think she's scattered or spread too thin. She's not. September is one of the most grace-filled women I've ever met. She brings me peace just talking to her, and I know she will for you as well. When I thought and prayed about who I wanted to contribute to this chapter of *Praying Mom*, I just knew she was the right person. Read her story and I think you'll agree.

Sometimes it takes a crisis moment for me to realize I have been living in the frantic pull of life for way too long. With many children, work, homeschooling, ministry, travel, grandparenting—the list goes on—I have always had a difficult time fitting everything in. There were days I would forget to eat, get in exercise, or even just take a breather.

I couldn't really trade in my kids or my busy life for a free pass from responsibility or a nap, so the day-to-day battle to fit everything in eventually caught up with me. Looking back, I wish I'd had more wisdom piped into my life, more awareness of the imbalance of busy versus priority. The product of a misdirected busy life is crisis.

So here's my story, and it is my prayer that it will never be yours.

Every day began the same way. I would slowly open my eyes and dread what was coming next. The hustle, the noise, the needs, and no time or place for me to take a breather. I didn't dread my children's place and presence in my life, don't get me wrong. I just felt a level of anxiety about the overwhelming lack of control I was feeling, as there was always another thing calling my name, and I never seemed to find a space that called me to rest. Every day also ended the same way: with me headed to bed knowing that even after a full day of intention and focus, I was still leaving something undone.

The day I realized I had become the busy, impatient, angry mom was the day I knew that something had to change. And that something was me.

My older kids knew me as the "yelling mom." I know this was partly because of my exhaustion, and mainly because I had no idea that this communication level with my children had become my way to "cope" with the stress level of daily life. I had slowly chosen productivity over bearing fruit that had lasting impact.

Repeated long weeks of tension with my teen daughter, arguing, sending her to her room, her words sharply coming back when I knew I didn't have the capacity to handle them anymore, were the cherry on top of a life filled with nothing but busy. Her arguments had worn me down, and the day came when my voice escalated quickly to anger and saying words that still bother me. Her eyes grew icy and sad and she ran to her room, slamming her door. There I was, standing in shame and regret that I didn't see this coming. That I had allowed my busy life to become too full of Band-Aids on small problems, that the most important people I was so busy for were now hurt by my lack of love and self-control.

It was a life-changing moment for me as a mom. I realized it wasn't about my daughter, or anger, or even me. It was about how a negligence of intention with my time with the Lord had brought a torrent of problems I needed to fix.

I went to my knees next to my bed and cried out in repentance and a desperate need for wisdom and guidance. I then knocked on my daughter's door. Eventually, she muttered through tears and anger to come in. I walked over to her and embraced her with all I had, and began praying. We cried, we prayed, and we took years to restore a broken, now beautiful thing.

Before we dive into what I know you've all been waiting for—practical tips for developing or kicking off your prayer life—I'd like to share with you a simple method of prayer that I have fallen in love with over the years. We developed it at Million Praying Moms for our prayer journals, and it is deliberately designed to help you learn to pray God's Word (because, as I've said over and over, I truly believe it's the very best thing to pray). We call it the Think, Pray, Praise Method of Prayer.

The Think, Pray, Praise Method of Prayer

In chapter 2, I told you about the two verses I was inspired by as I learned to pray God's Word. They are really the reason I started doing it. I would go so far as to say that I had no real knowledge or understanding about prayer when I started, but there were two things I knew to be true, and they form the foundation upon which I build my prayer life.

1. The Word of God is "living and active, sharper than any two-edged sword, piercing to the division of soul and of spirit, of joints and of marrow, and discerning the thoughts and intentions of the heart" (Hebrews 4:12 ESV).

2. The Word of God "shall not return to me [God] empty, but it shall accomplish that which I purpose, and shall succeed in the thing for which I sent it" (Isaiah 55:11 ESV).

These two verses are often the ones I go to when I teach other women to pray because they make things crystal clear and they aren't really rocket science. They simply offer a practical, biblical foundation for praying the Word of God over yourself or the people you love. Let me walk you through it step by step.

THINK

If I believe Hebrews 4:12—that God's Word is living and active and able to work to change me and my family to be more like Christ—then I simply need to start with thinking deeply about a Bible verse or passage God leads me to focus on. But how do you come up with the right one? Here's a process that has always worked for me when I needed help getting started.

Many, many times over my parenting years, I've sat down with a notebook or blank prayer journal and written down the sin struggles or character traits I want God to work on in each of my children. Some of the words on this list have changed as my children have grown, but surprisingly, some have stayed the same. This makes sense to me because I know that as a maturing believer, I don't struggle with all the things I did as a young believer. But there are some character flaws I've carried for a lifetime. Still, I won't give up on praying for victory in these areas for my kids in the same way I know God won't give up on working in me.

What does this mean for us as moms? Prayer requires consistent perseverance. Don't be discouraged if God doesn't answer you the way you want right away. Remember, God works on a timetable that is His own, not ours.

After making my list, I open the concordance in the back of my Bible and begin looking for verses or passages that mention each item on the list, and I look them up to make sure they really are talking about what I'm looking for. I usually try to pick just one verse or passage per item on the list. Once that part is done, I take some time to reflect on, process, and meditate over each verse. If I have time, I read a few verses that come before and after the verse, or even the entire chapter of the Bible, so I can have the proper context from which to understand it.

It's important to consider what God is speaking to our hearts through His Word and through the verses He leads us to. Dream about the future and what it might look like to see the message of this verse come to fruition in your life or your children's lives. In a small way, analyze the verse and figure out what you're inspired to pray from it. I always like to write these thoughts and my prayers that go with them down in a prayer journal. When I've filled up one journal, I lock it away in my grandfather's U.S. Navy chest for safekeeping, and then start a new one.

PRAY

My desire has been to allow my prayers to be inspired by God's Word. I try very hard not to take verses out of context or use them for a purpose or meaning other than what God intended for them. (Reading a verse in context really helps me with this. It's very important not to just pray what you hope that verse means, or what you'd like it to mean, but to keep in mind what it actually means.) Once I've selected a verse, I craft it into a prayer. Sometimes I stay as word-for-word as I can and then pray that verse back to God. Other times I work from the Think section of my journal and let my thoughts about that verse inspire how I pray it. But I'm always true to what I believe God meant for that verse to communicate to readers hundreds of years after it was written. If I need help with this, I consult Bible apps or commentaries. This is the best way I can ensure God will be true to His Word. God is under no obligation to fulfill it any other way than how He originally intended it, so ask Him to help you understand it before you pray it. If you need inspiration, go back to the prayers at the end of each chapter, or look at the Scripture-inspired prayers in part 2 of this book.

PRAISE

Think of praise like physically putting on a pair of rose-colored glasses. It literally changes the way you see the world around you, and I promise, once you've spent time in the Think and Pray part of this model, you'll have plenty of things to praise God for.

Ann Voskamp says, "The brave who focus on all things good and all things beautiful and all things true, even in the small, who give thanks for it and discover joy even in the here and now, they are the change agents who bring the fullest Light to all the world."[1]

When we pause to deliberately reflect on the good things God is doing in our lives right now—even the tiniest of things that might be difficult to see—it changes everything. Instead of focusing on all we don't have or don't like, gratitude for what we do have begins to bloom in our hearts, truly making us joyful. Each day I try to write down just a few things I'm grateful for, praising God for His continuous work of grace in my life! You'll be amazed at how this process works to breathe joy into your life.

The process of cultivating a habit of prayer doesn't have to be hard, but I really do believe it has to be done. If you've come to this book feeling a lack of power, strength, and energy in your spiritual life, I believe prayer is the answer. I know that's a strong statement, but I've experienced the truth of it in my own life. God really does draw near to us when we draw near to Him (James 4:8). Today, instead of allowing your lack of time, lack of energy, lack of mental capacity, or lack in general keep you from prayer, let it drive you to prayer. Make the mental shift to begin seeing those things as reasons to pray, not reasons to delay or neglect prayer.

And now for your practical tips! Below you'll find a mixture of tips for making time for your most important relationship, and tips for things you can do to make prayer a natural rhythm of your home so that your kids grow up in the habit of asking God for everything they need.

Practical Tips for a Vibrant Prayer Life

1. **Do *something*.** Scrape for it. Scratch for it. Act like your life depends on it, because in a very real way, it does. Be willing to do whatever it takes to get the time you need with your Creator as often as possible.
2. **Create an atmosphere you'll look forward to.** I love to pray in one of two spots every morning—my green prayer chair or the kitchen table. Sometimes, if the

weather is irresistible, I'll sit out on the back porch. I also like to diffuse my favorite essential oil blend while I'm praying (wild orange, Douglas fir, and peppermint). I pray off-and-on all day, but the biggest chunk of time I spend praying is in the morning before the kids get up, or sometimes just after they've left for school. Diffusing this same blend morning after morning not only helps wake up my brain, but I've used it for so long that my brain actually associates it with time to pray. I look forward to that smell every morning!

3. **"Brain dump" before you start.** If you're one of those people who wakes up thinking obsessively about all the things you have to do that day, it can help to make a quick to-do list or brain dump before you start praying. Write down everything you can think of that needs to be done that day, or even that week, so that when it pops back in your head to distract you while you're trying to pray, you don't have to worry about it. This can be one of the single greatest things to do that promotes concentration and eliminates distraction for praying moms!
4. **Prepare your heart.** One of my favorite things to pray, even before I get out of bed (if I can remember), is my Wake-Up Prayer (see appendix 1). I find that it really sets the tone for my day and even how I approach God as I sit down to pray and be in His Word.
5. **Find creative times.** I know I like to do the bulk of my praying in the morning, but I've also been known to pray myself to sleep at night. It's much easier and simpler than it might sound. All I do is ask the Lord to

bring to mind the people I need to pray for, and then I pray for them, one after the other, until I fall asleep. When I went back to work after my boys were born, I would often pray in the car or while I was pumping milk for them on my break. I prayed for them while I was rocking them to sleep at night and while I nursed them. Sometimes I would sing prayers over them while trying to quiet them down for a nap. If you're determined, there are limitless times to pray throughout the moments of your days. If you need specific help knowing what those moments are, dig deep into the Scripture-inspired prayers in part 2 of this book.

6. **Listen to an audio Bible.** One of my favorite ways to get the Word into my heart when my boys were very young was listening to an audio Bible. Some versions of Bible apps actually have someone reading the Scriptures to you. Listen to a few verses, turn it off, and then ask God how to pray in response to what you've just listened to.
7. **Have a "prayer street."** Amy Newsome, a women's ministry leader at First Baptist Church in Orlando, Florida, shared with me that her family had designated a specific road in their city as a "prayer street," and I thought this was a fantastic idea! Every time their family drives on this road, they pray about whatever is on their minds, or other prayer requests their family has.
8. **Have a set time to pray.** I have the alarm on my phone set to go off at 4:12 p.m. every single day so I can remember to pray at that time. For the past few months, I've been praying for healing for a family we know

whose son has tumors up and down his spine. I also pray for my kids at that time, my family, or the needs of the ministry. Whatever God puts on my heart.

9. **Pray "on the hours."** One of my favorite things to do when there's an urgent, pressing prayer need is to pray on the hours. Very simply, I set the alarm on my phone to go off every hour on the hour as a reminder to be persistent in prayer for a specific reason.
10. **Pray in the pick-up or drop-off line.** If your kids go to school, make sure your voice praying for them is the last thing they hear before going out into the world. I like to use the weekday Scripture-based prayers from Million Praying Moms as my inspiration for each day.
11. **Pray before games and performances or big test days.** Help your kids learn to invite God into the moments of their lives and begin to see that God cares about everything they care about.
12. **Leave your Bible lying open around the house.** If you have more than one Bible, leave them open (maybe to Psalms or Proverbs) around your house in strategic locations. When you're in that room, take a moment to look down and read a few verses. Pause to reflect on what they mean and how you can apply them to your life. Then pray for God to help you.
13. **Use a prayer resource that fits your season of life.** At Million Praying Moms, we've created an Everyday Prayers library of topical prayer journals just for busy moms like us. Use them to pray over a specific area of need for your child for the next twenty days.

14. **Have a prayer accountability partner.** It doesn't necessarily have to be someone who lives nearby. Really, it can be anyone who shares your passion to become a praying mom. Set up a check-in time every day when you commit to having prayed at least once.
15. **Pray while you're doing mundane chores.** Bring a little bit of the holy into the mundane (dishes, laundry, ironing, cleaning, etc.), and invite God to be a part of the moments of your day.
16. **Pray during playtime.** If you have a fenced-in backyard, let your littles go play for a few minutes while you sip your favorite warm beverage and enjoy a few minutes in prayer.
17. **Pray during kids' nap time.** If your children are still young and at home, consider praying while they're napping. If they're too old for a nap, think about instituting a consistent quiet time when you can read the Bible and pray for at least a few minutes.
18. **Pray out loud in your home.** I know there are people who find this difficult, but may I lovingly tell you to do it anyway? Your children will pattern their prayer lives after what they see and hear from you. Pray out loud.
19. **Make a prayer color chart.** For example, when you're in the car and see something blue, you remind your children to pray for their teachers. When you see something yellow, you pray for their friends. When you see something red, you pray for the children at school or in your community who are sick or needy. When you see something purple, you pray for health . . . and so on. Make

a chart that makes sense for you and your family and go with it! If you homeschool, pray together at agreed-upon times of the day.

20. **Give up on perfect.** It will never be perfect. If you expect perfect, you'll be disappointed every time. Relax your expectations. Take deep breaths. Start.

I sincerely hope these tips serve as a springboard to jump-starting your new or refreshed prayer life! Now, let's close out this chapter by turning to the rest of September's story.

I needed help in knowing how to make my time with the Lord a priority, and one that allowed me a space to present my busy life, my needs, my praises, and my motherhood before Him. I knew the solution, but I didn't know how to make it a new normal.

Life was still busy, so I realized I needed something planned and ready for me. I began praying Proverbs and Psalms over my days. It also helped me to read written prayers of motherhood from moms who have gone before me, so I would read Psalms or Proverbs out loud and then move to the written prayers.

Not only was reading Scripture and praying it over my children a delight, it was hope-filled and gave me a new perspective. I then began adding praying with my children in the mornings. This would help my heart to be tender to them, realizing they are waking up also to a world of new problems and possibilities and we are in this together with Jesus.

Praying when we wake, while working, and while living a life of motion brings a stillness or rest to your daily motherhood moments, by the sheer presence and knowledge of the Lord.

My children have seen prayer change me and change our lives. My life is *still* busy, but my order of pursuits and my path to resolving problems were changed by God's constant presence and reminder that there is always a better way. My youngest four children would not have recognized the mom raising their first six siblings. The fruit of prayer-filled days, humility, and the work of the Holy Spirit convicting and changing me over the years has reaped lasting fruit.

Pray It Forward

» The pride of accomplishment or making ourselves the hero of busy seamlessly weaves itself into the fabric of our hearts and lives until, without realizing, we think we can do this on our own. It is usually not on purpose, and almost always out of "survival" or trying to be all to everyone. But the bad fruit that comes with this is short words, anger, anxiety, impatience, and the list goes on.

» Don't wait for the crisis moments to make a change in the busyness.

» Prayer transforms your motherhood, because your time with Him changes you and your outlook on what is to come.

» Begin with writing out your heart-prayers for each child.

» Move to the places of wrestling you feel and write those words next.

» Open your Bible and pray the psalmists' words, as well as Proverbs, for your family.
» Pray with your children before school at the drop-off line.
» Stop when you feel rushed and remind yourself that stress and exhaustion only lead to one place: an unpredictable response when crisis arises. And it will. So make prayer the predictable place in your life. He promises He will always be there.

Prayers

Verse: "If any of you lacks wisdom, you should ask God, who gives generously to all without finding fault, and it will be given to you" (James 1:5 NIV).

Prayer: Father, help me remember to turn to you for help. In my chaos, I sometimes forget you're even there, but you've promised to never leave me, so I know you are. Move in my heart to create an awareness of my need and a desire to call on you for wisdom.

Verse: "My grace is sufficient for you, for my power is perfected in weakness" (2 Corinthians 12:9).

Prayer: Jesus, I don't like feeling weak. Everything in me wants to feel strong and like I have it all together, but I don't. Your Word says being weak is the best place I can be because it gives your strength room to win the day. I don't understand it, but I pray it would be true in my life.

Verse: "Come to me, all of you who are weary and burdened, and I will give you rest" (Matthew 11:28).

Prayer: Lord, I am weary and burdened. You are my relief. Help me to find rest in your Word and in your presence today, even if just for a few moments.

Part Two

Scripture-Inspired Prayers for Today's Christian Mom

This is my favorite section of the book. I hope it will be yours too.

Several months ago, Erin Mohring and I did an entire series on the *Million Praying Moms* podcast called "Everyday Prayers." Our goal with this series was to help you bring prayer into the everyday "normal" parts of your day, like a prayer for cooking dinner, or a prayer for wisdom and discernment, or even a prayer for your child's future spouse! From that podcast series, we developed an entire line of topical prayer journals called Everyday Prayers.

I want to share a similar collection of Scripture-inspired prayers here so you can use them as a reference and motivator to start praying right away. They are organized in the top ten areas where I believe moms can focus their prayers and feel like their efforts are worth it right away. There are five prayers for each topic. You can pray them all together, pray them throughout your day, or just refer to them as you need them. You might even find that one becomes your favorite and find yourself praying it on a regular basis. There aren't any rules with these prayers, so use them as they best fit your life. You can also visit www.millionprayingmoms.com/praying-mom-prayers to hear me pray them out loud over you and your family. I offer this to you as an exclusive gift because when I first started to pray more often, it was helpful to have a friend whose prayers I could model. Listening to others pray over the years has shaped the way my prayers sound and even what I say. I hope you'll find these useful.

This is your starting point. Pull these prayers out of the book, cut them up, and tape them in various places and spaces throughout your home. Or write them on sticky notes (that's how I first started praying), and begin memorizing them. (You can also print them out from the same site mentioned in the previous paragraph.) When you have the time, read the Scripture references for each prayer and seek to understand what you're praying. Write down your thoughts in a blank prayer journal as you go. But just pray, okay?

We've tried to give you thoughtful prayers that represent the heart of a mom—her concerns, fears, questions, and everyday needs. We promise that it will make a difference. We make that promise because we're living proof, and there's nothing special about us that God would withhold from you.

Now, go pray!

Prayers for When You Need Hope

1 Peter 5:10

"And after you have suffered a little while, the God of all grace, who has called you to his eternal glory in Christ, will himself restore, confirm, strengthen, and establish you." (ESV)

God of all grace, restore me with hope in you. Confirm to me over and over again that your Word is true, and that you're faithful to work it for good in my life. I'm weak, Lord. Perfect your strength in me, and establish me and my home for your glory. In Jesus' name, amen.

Ephesians 1:18

". . . having the eyes of your hearts enlightened, that you may know what is the hope to which he has called you, what are the riches of his glorious inheritance in the saints." (ESV)

Father, I can't see your hope right now. My circumstances make it cloudy and distorted, but I know it's there. Open my eyes and help me see. Help me remember that this world and its troubles are just a blip on the radar of time, and keep my eyes and heart fixed on the inheritance that's mine because I'm your child. In Jesus' name, amen.

Isaiah 40:31

"But they who wait for the LORD shall renew their strength; they shall mount up with wings like eagles; they shall run and not be weary; they shall walk and not faint." (ESV)

Lord, I feel like I'm constantly running ahead of you or falling behind. Help me to wait on you . . . to know that I know your will and to walk in it, confident that your strength will uphold me. Help me pursue you with all that I have and wait with expectation on your help and restoration. In Jesus' name, amen.

Philippians 1:6

"And I am sure of this, that he who began a good work in you will bring it to completion at the day of Jesus Christ." (ESV)

Lord, most of the time I feel very uncertain, but your Word tells me I can have complete certainty. Help me to submit my feelings to your truth and believe that you're still working in me and my family to accomplish your good plan. In Jesus' name, amen.

Psalm 33:18

"Behold, the eye of the LORD is on those who fear him, on those who hope in his steadfast love." (ESV)

*Father, you see your children—*El Roi *is your name: the God who sees. You aren't off in heaven wondering what's happening to me. Your eyes are on me, and you are working all things for my good and your glory. Help me to place all of my hope not on worthless things, but on your steadfast, unfailing love. In Jesus' name, amen.*

9

Prayers for When Your Child Needs Help

Psalm 31:2

"Incline your ear to me; rescue me speedily! Be a rock of refuge for me, a strong fortress to save me!" (ESV)

Father, please hear my cry for help. Turn your ear to us and bring help for our child. Surround ________________ (your child's name) with your strong protection, and be a refuge for our family in this time of need. In Jesus' name, amen.

Isaiah 41:10

"Fear not, for I am with you; be not dismayed, for I am your God; I will strengthen you, I will help you, I will uphold you with my righteous right hand." (ESV)

Father, I love ______________ (your child's name) so much, and my fears feel out of control. Help me place my trust in you. You are my God, and I need your touch. My strength is failing, but yours never does. Strengthen me now, help me, and uphold our family with your strong hand as we walk through this trial. In Jesus' name, amen.

Exodus 14:14

"The LORD will fight for you, and you have only to be silent." (ESV)

Father, I confess that I want to fix what's happening in my child's life. I never want _______________ (your child's name) to hurt when there's something I can do to make it stop. But I also know you love _______________ (your child's name) more than I do, and that you can use these circumstances as a part of his/her redemption story . . . as a part of his/her testimony. Help me to discern when I need to act, and when I need to sit still, be silent, and trust you with the fight. In Jesus' name, amen.

Proverbs 3:5–6

"Trust in the LORD with all your heart, and do not lean on your own understanding. In all your ways acknowledge him, and he will make straight your paths." (ESV)

Father, I acknowledge you as the Creator of the universe. You hold all things in your hands, including _______________ (your child's name). Help me to relax in the knowledge that you see the big picture. Help us to know what next step to take on the path you've chosen for us. In Jesus' name, amen.

Psalm 121:1–8

"I lift up my eyes to the hills. From where does my help come? My help comes from the LORD, who made heaven and earth. He will not let your foot be moved; he who keeps you will not slumber. Behold, he who keeps Israel will neither slumber nor sleep. The LORD is your keeper; the LORD is your shade on your right hand. The sun shall not strike you by day, nor the moon by night. The LORD will keep you from all evil; he will keep your life. The LORD will keep your going out and your coming in from this time forth and forevermore." (ESV)

Lord God, there is no rescue here on earth that compares to the plans you have for ______________ (your child's name). You are the Maker of heaven and earth, and you never sleep on the job. Keep ____________ (your child's name) from evil, and guard his/her life. Keep him/her safe under the shade of your mighty right hand. In Jesus' name, amen.

Prayers for When You Need More Joy

James 1:2–3

"Count it all joy, my brothers, when you meet trials of various kinds, for you know that the testing of your faith produces steadfastness." (ESV)

Lord, it isn't in my nature to be glad when trials come, but I want to be steadfast, trustworthy, and useful to you. I want my life to be a beacon of hope and a testimony of your grace and goodness. Help me to trust that even this trial is overflowing with your purpose for the building of your kingdom. In Jesus' name, amen.

Romans 15:13

"May the God of hope fill you with all joy and peace in believing, so that by the power of the Holy Spirit you may abound in hope." (ESV)

God of hope, fill me to overflowing with the joy of just knowing you. May that kind of joy trump every other. Fill me with peace as I choose to believe your promises are true. Let my hope spill over everyone around me. In Jesus' name, amen.

Hebrews 12:2

". . . looking to Jesus, the founder and perfecter of our faith, who for the joy that was set before him endured the cross, despising the shame, and is seated at the right hand of the throne of God." (ESV)

Father, my ultimate joy is found in the knowledge of what you did to save me and give me peace with you. When life's circumstances offer me little to be joyful about, I still have this, and because you have taken care of this, my greatest need, I can trust you to take care of everything else. In Jesus' name, amen.

Psalm 16:11

"You make known to me the path of life; in your presence there is fullness of joy; at your right hand are pleasures forevermore." (ESV)

Truly, Lord, this world has nothing to offer me in comparison to the joy of my salvation. When I'm tempted to despair, help me find joy in the simple pleasure of being in your company, and as I stay there, show me the path I need to take. In Jesus' name, amen.

Psalm 16:8–9

"I have set the LORD always before me; because he is at my right hand, I shall not be shaken. Therefore my heart is glad, and my whole being rejoices; my flesh also dwells secure." (ESV)

It is so easy to fix my eyes on the things of the world. Father, convict me of this, and show me when I'm doing it so that I can choose to keep you as my focus every day. May my heart be glad and may that gladness well up into worship because my salvation is secure in you. In Jesus' name, amen.

11

Prayers for When You're Angry

James 1:20

"For the anger of man does not produce the righteousness of God." (ESV)

Father, help me not to mistake my righteousness for yours. Make me a woman who loves you more than I love getting my own way. Help me to be patient and to show your love to those in my life who most need it. In Jesus' name, amen.

Ephesians 4:26–27

"Be angry and do not sin; do not let the sun go down on your anger, and give no opportunity to the devil." (ESV)

Lord, help me to be a self-controlled woman who can rationally and lovingly pursue reconciliation with you and with others. Help me lay myself aside and think more highly of the needs of others. Help me not to be easily offended and to let love for you and love for others be my guide. In Jesus' name, amen.

James 1:19

"Know this, my beloved brothers: let every person be quick to hear, slow to speak, slow to anger." (ESV)

Father, make me a listener. Help me choose to listen first, seeking to understand, and then speak. Give me a heart of compassion for those around me whose stories matter as much as my own. Let me be a woman who loves others well. In Jesus' name, amen.

Proverbs 29:11

"A fool gives full vent to his spirit, but a wise man quietly holds it back." (ESV)

Lord, sometimes I just need time to process my emotions. Often, when I take a step back from them, the bigger picture becomes clearer and my emotions change. Help me not to unleash my words or anger on those around me before I've taken them to you and considered all that I can't see. In Jesus' name, amen.

Proverbs 19:11

"Good sense makes one slow to anger, and it is his glory to overlook an offense." (ESV)

Father, make me a woman who has good sense! Help me be able to read the situations I'm in and respond in a way that brings you glory and helps others see you in me. Help me to overlook small offenses and not to be easily angered. In Jesus' name, amen.

Prayers for When You're Worn-Out and Weary

Matthew 11:28–30

"Come to me, all who labor and are heavy laden, and I will give you rest. Take my yoke upon you, and learn from me, for I am gentle and lowly in heart, and you will find rest for your souls. For my yoke is easy, and my burden is light." (ESV)

My soul needs rest, Father. I confess that the burdens I carry feel heavy and hard, so I know I need to lay them down at your feet. Help me learn how to bear this weight so that my life draws others to you. Be gentle with me, Lord, and help me rest. In Jesus' name, amen.

Isaiah 40:28–29

"Have you not known? Have you not heard? The LORD is the everlasting God, the Creator of the ends of the earth. He does not faint or grow weary; his understanding is unsearchable. He gives power to the faint, and to him who has no might he increases strength." (ESV)

God, you are everlasting. From the beginning of time, you have known that this weary season would come for me. I may be worn-out, but your unending power can sustain me and give me strength. I trust in you. In Jesus' name, amen.

1 Corinthians 10:13

"No temptation has overtaken you that is not common to man. God is faithful, and he will not let you be tempted beyond your ability, but with the temptation he will also provide the way of escape, that you may be able to endure it." (ESV)

Lord, protect me from believing I'm alone, or that what I'm experiencing is somehow unique. When I'm tempted to believe you're isolating me or being unfair, help me to instead believe you are faithful. In Jesus' name, amen.

Isaiah 40:1–2

"Comfort, comfort my people, says your God. Speak tenderly to Jerusalem, and cry to her that her warfare is ended, that her iniquity is pardoned, that she has received from the LORD's hand double for all her sins." (ESV)

Father, I believe you are the Redeemer of all things, and that you specialize in taking what's broken and making it beautiful. You are a tender Father, and you love me and my family, offering mercy when we're weary. In Jesus' name, amen.

2 Thessalonians 3:13

"As for you, brothers, do not grow weary in doing good." (ESV)

Why is it, Lord, that doing the right thing can be so hard? Help me rely on your strength when mine runs dry. Lord, as I encounter controversies, challenges, and even adversaries to the good work you've called me to do, help me remember that you alone are the one I live to please. In Jesus' name, amen.

Prayers for When You're Afraid

Isaiah 35:4

"Say to those who have an anxious heart, 'Be strong; fear not! Behold, your God will come with vengeance, with the recompense of God. He will come and save you.'" (ESV)

Father, my heart is anxious, and I need to know you're near. I believe you will come. I believe you will come. I believe you will come and take care of my every need. By faith, I will be strong and not fear, because I believe you will come! In Jesus' name, amen.

John 14:27

"Peace I leave with you; my peace I give to you. Not as the world gives do I give to you. Let not your hearts be troubled, neither let them be afraid." (ESV)

Father, help me remember not to look for peace as the world wants to give it. This peace is worthless and fades quickly, while the peace you offer is priceless and lasts. Your Word says I don't have to let my heart be troubled or afraid, so now, in this moment, I choose you. I choose to believe you are in control and caring for my every need. In Jesus' name, amen.

Joshua 1:9

"Have I not commanded you? Be strong and courageous. Do not be frightened, and do not be dismayed, for the LORD your God is with you wherever you go." (ESV)

Lord, I don't like what's ahead of me. I don't want to go where I have to go or do what I have to do. It seems too hard for me alone, but I'm actually not alone. As a believer, I carry you with me wherever I go. Please help me be strong and courageous today, and to remember that you are with me no matter what. In Jesus' name, amen.

Psalm 23

"The LORD is my shepherd; I shall not want. He makes me lie down in green pastures. He leads me beside still waters. He restores my soul. He leads me in paths of righteousness for his name's sake. Even though I walk through the valley of the shadow of death, I will fear no evil, for you are with me; your rod and your staff, they comfort me. You prepare a table before me in the presence of my enemies; you anoint my head with oil; my cup overflows. Surely goodness and mercy shall follow me all the days of my life, and I shall dwell in the house of the LORD forever." (ESV)

(Note: When I'm afraid, I like to pray all of Psalm 23 as my prayer, especially verse four: "Even though I walk through the valley of the shadow of death, I will fear no evil, for you are with me; your rod and your staff, they comfort me." I

used to repeat this as a prayer over and over every night as I tried to go to sleep alone in my parents' house while they traveled. I can't improve on perfection, so I just pray it word for word.)

Psalm 27:1

"The Lord is my light and my salvation; whom shall I fear? The Lord is the stronghold of my life; of whom shall I be afraid?" (ESV)

(Note: This is another verse I pray word for word when I am afraid. I find it is perfect for going to sleep at night. I simply repeat it over and over again to remind myself that I belong to the Lord and nothing can touch me unless it comes through Him first. Again, no need to improve on perfection. Just pray the verse as is!)

Prayers for When You Need God to Move

1 John 5:14

"And this is the confidence that we have toward him, that if we ask anything according to his will he hears us." (ESV)

Lord, purify my heart and make it measure up against the truth of your Word so that I can come to you with clean hands, asking according to your will. I know you hear my prayers. Please come and make a way where there isn't one. In Jesus' name, amen.

1 Peter 3:12

"For the eyes of the Lord are on the righteous, and his ears are open to their prayer. But the face of the Lord is against those who do evil." (ESV)

Father, thank you for sending Jesus to take the punishment for my sin. I know that I have righteous standing before you because of HIS righteousness, not because of my own merit. It's from that place that I ask you to hear and act. Please send a miracle of some kind to help us. In Jesus' name, amen.

Psalm 40:17

"As for me, I am poor and needy, but the Lord takes thought for me. You are my help and my deliverer; do not delay, O my God!" (ESV)

Father, I have nothing to bring to the table except my faith in Jesus. I'm yours because of Him. We are desperate and needy and humbled before you. Please keep us near. Be our Savior today. Save us out of our challenge, and don't delay. In Jesus' name, amen.

Jeremiah 29:12–13

"Then you will call upon me and come and pray to me, and I will hear you. You will seek me and find me, when you seek me with all your heart." (ESV)

Lord, I come to you with my whole heart, seeking you on behalf of ____________________ (your child's name, or the situation). Hear my prayers. Help me to find you and follow you and trust you as we walk through this trial. In Jesus' name, amen.

Psalm 66:17–20

"I cried to him with my mouth, and high praise was on my tongue. If I had cherished iniquity in my heart, the Lord would not have listened. But truly God has listened; he has attended to the voice of my prayer. Blessed be God, because he has not rejected my prayer or removed his steadfast love from me!" (ESV)

Father, rid me of all iniquity. Cleanse me and hear my prayer. I praise you with all that is in me and cry out to you to attend my prayer. Thank you for not rejecting me or removing your love from me, even in this. In Jesus' name, amen.

Prayers for When You Need Strength to Make It

Psalm 28:7

"The Lord is my strength and my shield; in him my heart trusts, and I am helped; my heart exults, and with my song I give thanks to him." (ESV)

Father, I am weak, you are strong. My strength runs out. Yours never does. In you my heart trusts. I don't trust in myself but in your ability to give me what I need for this day. Help me to be thankful for all the gifts you give. In Jesus' name, amen.

Jeremiah 32:17

"Ah, Lord God! It is you who have made the heavens and the earth by your great power and by your outstretched arm! Nothing is too hard for you." (ESV)

Lord God, if you could create the heavens and earth from scratch, you have all the strength I need to be victorious in this day. Give me the strength I need to ______________ (fill in your need). Nothing is too hard for you, and I place myself wholeheartedly in your care! In Jesus' name, amen.

Psalm 59:16

"But I will sing of your strength; I will sing aloud of your steadfast love in the morning. For you have been to me a fortress and a refuge in the day of my distress." (ESV)

Father, you are a fortress around me. You go before me. You stand beside me. You are my refuge from the storm. As I walk through __________________ (your circumstances), may it be clear to everyone around me that it was your strength that brought victory, and not mine. Use this trial as a way to bring yourself glory! In Jesus' name, amen.

Psalm 119:28

"My soul melts away for sorrow; strengthen me according to your word!" (ESV)

Father, I know your Word holds the answer to my sorrow. I need you to come and give me the strength to open it. Show me where to go. Show me what to read. Your Word is living and active. Please make it alive in me and use it to bring strength to my soul. In Jesus' name, amen.

1 Chronicles 16:11

"Seek the LORD and his strength; seek his presence continually!" (ESV)

There is no healing apart from you, Lord Jesus. Your Word and your presence are a balm to my weariness. Help me to seek more of you, more of the time, so that I may find the strength I need in this sinful world. In Jesus' name, amen.

Prayers for When You're Sad

Matthew 5:4

"Blessed are those who mourn, for they shall be comforted." (ESV)

Father, the world seems dark and my vision narrow. I need the comfort and light of your presence to help me see. Send me your light, Lord. Help me see past the shadows and heaviness to the comfort and rest I have in you. In Jesus' name, amen.

Psalm 3:3

"But you, O LORD, are a shield about me, my glory, and the lifter of my head." (ESV)

Anything good about me comes from you, Lord God. Help me devote my life, no matter what, to glorifying you. Lift my head from this sadness and help me gaze upon you. Open my eyes to the shield you are for me and lead me in your truth. In Jesus' name, amen.

Isaiah 41:10

"Fear not, for I am with you; be not dismayed, for I am your God; I will strengthen you, I will help you, I will uphold you with my righteous right hand." (ESV)

Father, never let me forget how strong your hands really are. You hold all things together, including me. Let the magnitude of the words "I am your God" thrill me and uplift me because I belong to you, Lord. Strengthen my countenance because of who you are, and keep me safe in your hands. In Jesus' name, amen.

1 Peter 5:7

". . . casting all your anxieties on him, because he cares for you." (ESV)

Father, forgive me for forgetting how much it really means that you care for me. When life gets hard, it's easy to think no one cares, but in truth, the most important One cares. Right now, I offer you everything I've been carrying—everything weighing me down and causing me sadness—and trust the God who cares for my burdens. In Jesus' name, amen.

John 10:10

"The thief comes only to steal and kill and destroy. I came that they may have life and have it abundantly." (ESV)

Father, give me eyes to see the abundance in my life. Help me to see the rich gifts you have provided, even as I walk through this trial. In all things, help me to remember that my enemy wants me to focus on my lack and forget about your riches in Christ Jesus. Today, with your help, the enemy won't win my heart. In Jesus' name, amen.

Prayers for When You Need Peace

John 16:33

"I have said these things to you, that in me you may have peace. In the world you will have tribulation. But take heart; I have overcome the world." (ESV)

I don't know why I'm always so surprised when struggles come, because your Word is clear that they will. Today, Lord, I'll wash my heart and mind with the truth of your Word, because it is my only real source of peace. You have overcome, and therefore, so have I. May this knowledge follow me throughout the day and provide my soul with rest. In Jesus' name, amen.

2 Corinthians 13:11

"Finally, brothers, rejoice. Aim for restoration, comfort one another, agree with one another, live in peace; and the God of love and peace will be with you." (ESV)

Father, give me the heart of a peacemaker. Help me look at those around me as valuable and loved by you, even and especially when they're different from me. Guide me by your Spirit into compassionate understanding for others. Restore my difficult relationships. Make me a comforter so that I might live at peace with those around me and point others to you. In Jesus' name, amen.

Philippians 4:6–7

"Do not be anxious about anything, but in everything by prayer and supplication with thanksgiving let your requests be made known to God. And the peace of God, which surpasses all understanding, will guard your hearts and your minds in Christ Jesus." (ESV)

Help me in this moment, Lord, to give my anxiety over to you. In obedience to your Word, I bring ____________________ (your situation) to you and ask you to move. You are good and full of compassion, slow to anger, and full of mercy. You are my provider, my strong tower, and the lover of my soul. You saved me, redeemed me, and set my feet upon the Rock. When I'm tempted to be anxious, remind me of these truths so I can find peace in you. In Jesus' name, amen.

Colossians 3:15

"And let the peace of Christ rule in your hearts, to which indeed you were called in one body. And be thankful." (ESV)

Father, I pray that you would make the peace I have as your child, redeemed by the blood of Jesus, rule over any other emotional state I'm tempted to feel. When I feel a lack of peace, help me remember to look to you above all else. In Jesus' name, amen.

Isaiah 26:3

"You keep him in perfect peace whose mind is stayed on you, because he trusts in you." (ESV)

Jesus. Jesus. Jesus. I love to repeat your name. It's the name above all other names. The name that commands reverence and worship. I worship you now, Lord. Thank you for the gift of your Son. Help me to keep my mind on Him and His sacrifice for my soul at all times, especially when I need peace. In Jesus' name, amen.

Appendix One

The Wake-Up Prayer

I Am Surrendered.

I am weak. Lord, you are strong.
I have questions. You have the answers.
I will make mistakes. You make beauty from ashes.
I am broken. You specialize in restoration.
I will fall. You will uphold me with your Mighty Right Hand.
I will rejoice, because you made this day.
I will work at my calling with all my heart as if I'm working just for you.
I will let my light shine, pointing others to the light of Christ.
I will offer grace, because you gave grace to me.
I will love, because you first loved me.
I will forgive, because you are forgiving.
I will not fear, because you are faithful.

Today, I might fail, but I'm on the winning team. I surrender my hopes, dreams, pains, needs, and victories to your sovereign hand. Make me useful to your kingdom today, O Lord, and may this day in my life bring glory to you.

Appendix Two

The Way to Salvation

In case you've never met Jesus, let me tell you about Him. He's the One you need to know. Moving forward, I hope you'll define your life as before you met Him, and after. Jesus, my Jesus, is God's only Son. He was born to a virgin (Mary), and He lived thirty-three years on this earth without sinning against God. (You can verify His life and death; it's real history.) He faced every kind of temptation you and I face (at its root), and yet He lived a completely sinless life. Many followed Him, recognizing that the words He spoke were the keys to life. They believed in Him, were healed by Him, and loved Him. And then they turned on Him.

The religious leaders of the day were jealous of the way people followed Him and listened to Him instead of them, so they devised a wicked scheme to get Him arrested, falsely charged, and executed. He was stripped, beaten, spit on, and at the end, so horribly treated that He was physically unrecognizable. Then He was nailed to a cross—two wooden beams nailed together so that they would support a human body. The nails pierced through His hands and feet. He hung in agony on the cross, with the weight of my sin and yours laid fully on His shoulders until the debt had been paid, and then He died.

In the Old Testament temple, where God's people worshiped Him and offered sacrifices for their sin before Jesus came, there was a curtain that separated the Holy Place from the Most Holy Place, called the Holy of Holies. Behind that curtain was where the Ark of the Covenant was kept, and only the High Priest could enter it once a year to offer sacrifices for the sins of the people. So holy was this place that if anyone else dared to enter on any other day, they immediately died. Why? Because it represented the unblemished, completely clean, and pure presence of God. Exodus 33:20 teaches us that no one could look at God and live. Even Moses had to cover his face as God passed him by.

This curtain, or veil, represented the fact that human beings are utterly different from God, even though they are made in His image. It symbolized the separation of God from sinful mankind—a boundary, if you will, that only the High Priest could cross because God can't be in the presence of sin, and even then only this one time a year to atone for the sins of the people.

When Jesus died, the curtain, sixty feet long, was torn in the temple from top to bottom (Matthew 27:51). Completely torn, exposed, no longer able to keep God's people from getting to Him.

Jesus is the reason we can get close to God. Without Him, we are exposed and vulnerable. With Him, we can crawl right up into the lap of God and have a relationship with Him as our Father, because His sacrifice makes us clean. We no longer need a High Priest to enter in and make sacrifices for us. Jesus *was* the sacrifice, and no other sacrifice will ever be needed. Our sins no longer separate us from God, because Jesus took them upon himself. *It. Is. Finished.*

Scholars are undecided on it, but I believe when Jesus died, He actually went to hell for you and for me. After spending three days there, and after His broken earthly body had been buried in a tomb, God raised Him from the dead! The power of God triumphed over the power of sin once and for all, and now Jesus sits at the right hand of God in heaven, and lives in the hearts of individual believers, like me, and, I hope, like you.

It's a sensational story, really, but if God is working in your heart right now, you know it's true. And not just that it's true . . . you know it's true *for you*. Jesus, God's only Son, carried the weight of *your* sin on His shoulders as He was nailed to the cross. The full extent of God's wrath toward *your* sin was absorbed by Jesus, and when He rose from the dead, He made a way for you to be forgiven for all those things (sins) you've been holding on to, trying to make them right by yourself before coming to Him. Let Him take them? I promise, if you'll let go of the control, He'll take everything broken about you and make it whole. He might even use the very things you're worried about to draw other people to Him. All it takes is time. And if you're already a believer in Jesus, you can drop the baggage you're holding too. He wants to hold it for you and make something beautiful out of your brokenness. All you need to do is ask.

If you prayed the prayer for salvation for the first time, please reach out to me at millionprayingmoms@gmail.com so we can help you take the next steps!

Contributors

Sandra Peoples is a special-needs mom and sibling. She and her family live outside of Houston, Texas, where she serves her church as the director of special-needs ministry. She's the author of *Unexpected Blessings: The Joys and Possibilities of Life in a Special-Needs Family* and the host of the podcast *Self Care and Soul Care for the Caregiver*. You can connect with her at www.sandrapeoples.com.

Teri Lynne Underwood has a passion for helping others spend time in God's Word and grow in relationship with Him. She is the founder of Scripture Dig, a multigenerational community of women who study the Bible together. She is the creator of Scripture Dig for Kids, an inductive Bible study curriculum for children ages five to eleven, and the author of *Praying for Girls: Asking God for the Things They Need Most*. Connect with Teri Lynne at www.terilynneunderwood.com.

Stacey Thacker is an author, blogger, speaker, and believer who loves God's Word and connecting with women. Her passion is to encourage women in their walks with God and equip them to study the Bible. She created the blog community Mothers of Daughters and now blogs on her site, www.staceythacker.com. She's the author of six books, including *Hope for the Weary Mom: Let God Meet You in the Mess*, and wrote the Bible study series The Girlfriends' Guide to the Bible. She worked with Campus Crusade for Christ for five years before becoming a full-time mom to four daughters.

Gina Smith is a writer and author who has been married for thirty-one years to Brian, a college professor and athletic trainer. For the past twenty-plus years, Gina and her husband have served on a Christian college campus as the on-campus parents, and her husband has been a professor and dean of students. They live on the campus where they raised both of their now married children. In her spare time, Gina writes for several websites, and recently she authored her first book, *Grace Gifts: Practical Ways to Help Your Children Understand God's Grace*. She also writes at her blog: www.ginalsmith.com.

Connie Albers is a podcaster, author, and keynote speaker who is passionate about parenting and strengthening families. She is the author of *Parenting beyond the Rules: Raising Teens with Confidence and Joy*. Connie has five children and travels the country doing TV interviews, radio segments, speaking presentations, and strengths coaching. Connie spent twenty-five years working with teens and thirty years as a homeschool leader.

Suzanne Gosselin lives in California with her husband, Kevin, and four children. Formerly the editor of *Clubhouse Jr.* magazine, she is the author of multiple books and devotionals, including *Grit and Grace: Devotions for Warrior Moms*. Suzanne loves the beach, good coffee, and spending time with her husband and kids.

September McCarthy has been married to her husband, Dan, for thirty years. Together they have ten children and nine grandchildren. They have been homeschooling for more than two decades, and have launched six arrows, with four more still at home. September is the author of *Why Motherhood Matters* and directs a large homeschool cooperative in New York. She also cohosts a generational podcast, *Mom to Mom Podcast*, with Kate Battistelli and Jamie Erickson. September founded and owns September & Co., an online and vendor-based educational resource shop for families.

Acknowledgments

Cory: Always you. Not one single word would've made its way onto paper if it weren't for your support. I love you!

My boys: God has used you to produce the greatest lessons of my life. You're my favorites, and there is nothing you could ever do to make me not love you.

Jamie Soranno: Thank you for being willing to step out of your comfort zone to write the foreword for this book. I love your words. You should write more of them.

Heather Medvedenko, Debbie Harper, Susie Amos, Joan Colwell, and Deb Fann: I listened to you pray when God was first developing my prayer life, and it changed the way I pray and understand God. Thank you for setting an example.

Chip MacGregor: You've been exactly what I needed in an agent all these years. Thank you for respecting my calling, encouraging me to keep going, challenging me when my ideas were terrible, and for providing wise counseling for me and Million Praying Moms in so many ways.

Sandra, Teri Lynne, Stacey, Gina, Connie, Suzanne, and September: I knew I couldn't write this book by myself because I haven't experienced every challenge firsthand. I'm so grateful for your stories that gave life to the biblical concepts inside. Thank you for being vulnerable so that other women could benefit.

Gina and Brian Smith; Mike and Stephanie Mitchener: Thank you for reading these words before they were sent out into the world. I deeply appreciate your rich wisdom and diligent effort to make sure my theology isn't way out in left field.

Jeff Braun: Thanks for making me seem like a better writer than I am. You were a pleasure to work with on this project, but then you always are!

The Million Praying Moms family: You answered a simple question and sparked an entire book. I pray that it represents you well, and that God uses your willingness to answer an email to bless the lives of countless other moms.

My Jesus: You're the way, and I'm taking it. Thank you for patiently developing in me a greater and greater love for following you. I hope these words are a fragrant offering before your throne.

Notes

Chapter 1 I Don't Know If My Prayers Really Matter

1. Brooke McGlothlin, *Gospel-Centered Mom* (Colorado Springs: Multnomah, 2017), 56.

2. J. D. Greear, "Satan's Go-To Temptation Against You," Desiring God, August 3, 2018, https://www.desiringgod.org/articles/satans-go-to-temptation-against-you.

3. Timothy Keller, *Prayer: Experiencing Awe and Intimacy with God* (New York: Dutton, 2014), 26.

4. Marshall Segal, "What Difference Will Prayer Make?" Desiring God, January 13, 2020, https://www.desiringgod.org/articles/what-difference-will-prayer-make.

Chapter 2 I Don't Know What to Pray

1. Matthew Henry, *Matthew Henry Commentary on the Whole Bible (Complete)*, Vol. 3, 1706, Bible Study Tools, https://www.biblestudytools.com/commentaries/matthew-henry-complete/psalms/22.html.

2. John Piper, "In the Beginning Was the Word" sermon, Desiring God, September 21, 2008, https://www.desiringgod.org/messages/in-the-beginning-was-the-word.

3. Brooke McGlothlin, *How to Control Your Emotions So They Don't Control You* (Amazon Kindle, 2013).

4. John Piper, "Should I Use the Bible When I Pray?" Desiring God, September 28, 2007, https://www.desiringgod.org/interviews/should-i-use-the-bible-when-i-pray.

5. Mike Mitchener, "Balanced Christianity" sermon, October 11, 2020, https://www.riverviewtoday.org/sermons/sermon/2020-10-11/balanced-christianity.

Chapter 3 I'm Exhausted from Trying to Trust God

1. Elisabeth Elliot, "The Lord's Prayer Part 1," January 24, 1993 lecture, https://elisabethelliot.org/resource-library/lectures-talks/the-lords-prayer-part-1-2/.

2. Stacey Thacker, *Threadbare Prayer* (Nashville: Abingdon Press, 2020), 8.

Chapter 4 I Don't Believe God Hears My Prayers

1. Tim Keller, *Prayer: Experiencing Awe and Intimacy with God* (New York: Viking, 2014), 11.

2. Keller, 12.

3. Keller, 20, 30.

4. Corrie ten Boom, *The Hiding Place* (Bloomington, MN: Chosen Books, 2006), 209.

5. Ruth Bell Graham, "Ruth Bell Graham, How to Start Praying," *Decision* magazine, July 1, 2020, https://decisionmagazine.com/ruth-bell-graham-how-to-start-praying/.

6. Jon Bloom, "What to Do When We're Prayerless," Desiring God, January 23, 2015, https://www.desiringgod.org/articles/what-to-do-when-were-prayerless.

7. Elisabeth Elliot, "The Lord's Prayer Part 1," January 24, 1993 lecture, https://elisabethelliot.org/resource-library/lectures-talks/the-lords-prayer-part-1-2/.

8. Ibid.

9. Ibid.

10. Ibid.

11. Ibid.

Chapter 5 I Can't Pray until I Get My Life Together

1. Augustine, "Letters of St. Augustine, Letter 130," New Advent, https://www.newadvent.org/fathers/1102130.htm, accessed January 2020.

2. Paul Miller, *A Praying Life: Connecting with God in a Distracting World* (Colorado Springs: NavPress, 2017), 109.

3. John Piper, *Desiring God* (Colorado Springs: Multnomah, 2011), 161.

Chapter 6 I Have Small Children. I Can't Even Think, Much Less Pray!

1. Ruth Bell Graham, "Ruth Bell Graham: How to Start Praying," *Decision* magazine, July 1, 2020, https://decisionmagazine.com/ruth-bell-graham-how-to-start-praying/.

2. John Piper, "A Theology of Prayer in Three Minutes," Desiring God, February 28, 2013, https://www.desiringgod.org/interviews/a-theology-of-prayer-in-three-minutes.

3. Brooke McGlothlin, *Gospel-Centered Mom* (Colorado Springs: Multnomah, 2017), 31; Chuck Swindoll quote from *Moses: A Man of Selfless Dedication, Great Lives from God's Word* (Nashville: Thomas Nelson, 1999), 68.

4. Elisabeth Elliot, "The Lord's Prayer, Part 1," January 24, 1993 lecture, https://elisabethelliot.org/resource-library/lectures-talks/the-lords-prayer-part-1-2/.

5. R. A. Torrey, *The Power of Prayer and the Prayer of Power* (Grand Rapids, MI: Fleming H. Revell, 1924), 106.

Chapter 7 I'm So Busy!

1. Ann Voskamp, *One Thousand Gifts* (Nashville: Thomas Nelson, 2011), 58.

Brooke McGlothlin has encouraged thousands of moms toward a richer prayer life for over a decade. She is the co-founder of Million Praying Moms, a popular online ministry that exists to help moms make prayer their first and best response to the challenges of parenting. Brooke is the author of several books and resources for moms and lives in the Appalachian Mountains of southwest Virginia with her husband and their two sons.

Also from Brooke McGlothlin

Learn how to fight for your son's heart in prayer with this encouraging book! Filled with uplifting stories, biblical wisdom, and specific prayers straight from the Bible, *Praying for Boys* equips you to effectively bring your biggest concerns for your son before God so you can raise a godly man. Includes a 21-day prayer guide for small groups, in person or online.

Praying for Boys